Running the Crim

STORIES FROM THE
COOLEST RACE IN MICHIGAN

Running the Crim

STORIES FROM THE
COOLEST RACE IN MICHIGAN

ANTHONY R. ELLIS, M.D.

Running Brain
Mine's running. Is yours?

Running the Crim
Stories from the Coolest Race In Michigan
Edited and compiled by Anthony R. Ellis, M.D.
First edition printed 2005 in the U.S.A

ISBN, print ed.   0-9770509-0-4
ISBN, PDF ed.   0-9770505-1-2

LIBRARY OF CONGRESS CONTROL NUMBER 2005905675

This book is for entertainment purposes only. Always check with your doctor before starting any new exercise regimen. Every effort has been made to provide complete and accurate information. The information is provided on an "as-is" basis. The editor and publisher shall have neither liability nor responsibility to any person or entity with respect to any loss or damages arising from the information contained in this book.

Mention of specific companies, organizations, or authorities in this book does not imply their endorsement of this book. All terms mentioned in this book that are known to be trademarks or service marks have been appropriately capitalized. The publisher cannot attest to the accuracy of this information. Use of a term in this book should not be regarded as affecting the validity of any trademark or service mark.

While the Crim Festival of Races, Inc. offered assistance by way of providing access to publicly viewed documents and photographs, nothing contained herein should be viewed or determined to be any approval or authorization by the Crim or any of its agents or representatives. All material contained herein, all statements made and opinions expressed are from those individuals and are not the official word of the Crim, nor the viewpoint of the Crim.

Because a majority of the information is provided through personal accounts of individuals regarding events in their lives as they remember them, the information is subject to the foibles of memory. In addition, these accounts were edited for spelling, punctuation, grammar, and interest, and as such, are not exactly as they were originally submitted. All efforts were made to preserve the contributors' original content and message.

Published by: Running Brain
P.O. Box 320074
Flint Township, MI 48532
1-866-WHY-I-RUN
www.RunningBrain.com

Mine's running. Is yours?

Notable Quotes

In the nylon-short running era, races were the final exams. Each participant toed the line with one thought in mind: How do I get this race over as quickly as possible? These days, races are the commencement ceremony that makes all of the training worth it. The races are celebrations shared by athletes of all abilities. More than any other event, the Crim provides the opportunity for celebration and the joy of accomplishment for every participant in every race. Whether you are just entering the running community or are a seasoned veteran, you'll find that you can succeed and have your success embraced at the Crim.

— John "the Penguin" Bingham
Runner's World columnist, and best-selling author

Since the summer of 1977, the Crim has become a much loved treasure of the Flint Community—truly the biggest event in town. However, the real essence of this race goes beyond the fanfare and hoopla of a world-class running event. At the heart of the Crim are thousands of individual success stories and personal triumphs. Many stories are truly inspirational. This race has taken on legendary status for those men and women who have taken part over the past twenty-eight years. All it takes is one race, one year, and the Crim experience will hook you for life!

— Deb Kiertzner
Crim Race Director 2005

VOICES OF CRIM RUNNERS

I made it to the sidewalk, sat down, and took off my saturated Trax shoes, which must have weighed six pounds apiece. The cheap insoles were made of cardboard and had disintegrated into pulp. As I sat feeling bad about the loss of my shoes, the last few runners came in. A cheer went up for a haggard old man wearing of all things white dress shoes with platform heels. — Riley McLincha

On the Saginaw Street bricks, my husband popped out of the crowd yelling and cheering, so we ran flat out to the end, gave our best mug to the camera, and stepped on the finish line together. Much to my amazement, hundreds of people were with us. We didn't finish dead last! It was so much fun. — Lenke Kratochvil

Over the years, the Crim has helped me develop the skills needed to be successful in all areas of life. I've learned how to overcome obstacles, be persistent, and realize that being a small part of something can add up to something much greater. — Dan Miglin

Life is unbelievably large and can seem arbitrary, sometimes. How nice it is to discover that we are in a bigger race with people who are more like us than different. Being a group leader has taught me that each of us has a story. If I listen hard for these stories, I can hear them.
— Brian Barkey

Gym class was my nemesis all my school life. I was the first kid out when playing dodge ball, the last kid picked for every team. If you were to ask me prior to 2001, I would have bet you *any* money that I would never ever run, unless someone big was chasing me. — Shari Ellis

The Crim is a bond that brings all of us together, not just the runners, but also all the wonderful volunteers and all those fantastic supporters along the course.
— Malissa Lauderbaugh

In the end, though, running the Crim isn't something you do for other people. It certainly isn't something you do for glory. There isn't an age group old enough for me to ever win. It's hard to explain the joy, satisfaction, and sense of well being it brings. I just know it does. — Mike Laux

As a retired Special Education teacher, I saw the benefits of Special Olympics for some of my students. I can certainly appreciate the financial support the Crim race has given to this very worthy cause. Long live the Crim!
— Karen J. Bell

I came home and said to my husband with a disappointed sound, "We *only* did four miles tonight." When I realized those words had come out of *my* mouth, I was shocked. *I had changed!* — Barbara Besso

Try to imagine the luck, the skill, and the ability that has enabled them to walk up to the starting line and run ten miles for more than twenty-five years in a row. Injuries and illness have come and gone, rainstorms and hellish heat have not stopped them. — John Jerome

The Crim is not just the "Coolest Race In Michigan." In my book, it is *the* coolest race, period. It has become part of my heart. How long will I keep up my consecutive streak? My goal is fifty consecutive years. I'll check back with you in 2044 and fill you in! — Allison Ensign

I was over forty, recovering from cancer, and had never run a day in my life. When I went home and casually announced over dinner that I was going to run the Crim, my eleven-year-old daughter suggested that perhaps the surgeons had removed a good portion of my brain... — Deb Kiertzner

I kept running, winning, and smoking. As do all serious runners, I subscribed to *Runner's World,* and learned that if I could quit smoking I could gain ten percent oxygen uptake and possibly run faster. That was it. Goodbye cigarettes, hello serious running competition. — Bob Daly

Dedicated to my wife, Shari
For my daughters,
Alaina, Serena, and Mia

In memory of Shahin Manzari,
Whose story inspired this book

TABLE OF CONTENTS

INTRODUCTION

This book is not about how to cut five minutes off your personal best. You won't find a chapter on how to run the Crim like a Kenyan champion. I have many running books that tell me how to run fast. You probably do, too. This book is about ordinary runners, regular folk. We asked Crim runners to write down and send in their personal reflections on the Crim experience and how it changed them.

The stories contained in this book tell of people setting goals, overcoming fears, and changing their lives. These personal accounts explain why the Crim isn't just another race. These stories of transformation prove that running isn't about pain, self-torture, fatigue, and injuries. It's about joy, laughter, fun, and new friends. Something is addictive about the Crim, an addiction that brings out the best in the people who discover the race.

This book is about why we run and how running changes us for the better. It's about the best road race in Michigan and the effect of the Crim Festival of Races on the people and the runners who participate. Here are the ninety percent of runners who run for fun and fitness. They run because they enjoy the events and hanging around other runners. Many of our best friends are runners just like us. We run because we love it or because we want to know what all the fuss is about. Some of us run for peace of mind or because running is a part of us. Others run to cope with loss or pain. We all have our reasons. The Crim is there for everyone and so are the roads, trails, and races all over the United States and the world.

The editing and compilation of these stories was a labor of love for a race that turned me into one of these ordinary runners. The overall effects of beginning to run have been anything but ordinary. Before I joined the Crim Training Program I was overweight and out of shape. Now I'm in the best shape of my life, I feel great, and I have more to give to my patients, family, and friends. I look forward to running each week with our training group because of the friendships and running camaraderie. My wife and I now choose vacation spots by the quality and availability of running roads and trails at the destination. That's quite a change from being a potato-chip-eating couch potato who always took the elevator.

I hope you enjoy this book, and I would be happy to hear from you. I hope this book inspires you to become a runner or walker. If the spirit moves you, don't miss the **C**oolest **R**ace **I**n **M**ichigan or the equivalent in your neck of the woods. Sign up and run or walk with a friend. If you have a running story or a Crim story and want to share it with others, send them to me. I'm always looking for a good story. There may be a sequel to this book.

Anthony R. Ellis, M.D.
c/o Running Brain
P.O. Box 320074
Flint Township, MI 48532
E-mail your stories to me at:
TheTaoRunner@yahoo.com

ACKNOWLEDGMENTS

There are always many people to thank when a book is created. I would like to thank the following people, without whom this idea would not have borne fruit.

Shirin Manzari inspired me with her emotional account of why she ran the Crim. My wife, Shari, had the initial idea of collecting stories like Shirin's from the Crim Training Program. Shari has been supportive throughout the process and has been my muse. Brian and Dorie Barkey provided enthusiasm in the planning phase and put me in touch with key people at the Crim organization to get the project started. Sherlynn Everly, the former race director of the Crim Festival of Races, believed in me and presented the idea to the Crim Board when she knew nothing about me except that I was a Crim runner. Deb Kiertzner, the current race director, and Gerry Myers, the CEO of the Crim Festival of Races, picked up where Sherlynn left off and saw the book through to completion. The Crim organization gave me access to its logos, press releases, photos, and Crim facts, and helped make the finished book available at races. Without the Crim staff there would be no Crim Festival and no stories or fond memories.

Thanks also to Brian Barkey and Riley McLincha for their excellent submissions and for getting the word out to runners that brought in many of the stories in the book.

Special thanks are in order for my running group (they know who they are) for not telling me to shut up when I gave them updates on the progress of the book. They continue to provide friendship, motivation, and support. They are a source of great joy in my life.

I would also like to thank Jeff Galloway and John "the Penguin" Bingham for their support and for developing and popularizing a way for ordinary folks to get involved in and enjoy running. Without the Galloway "run/walk" approach, and the Bingham "waddle on" philosophy, I would have ended up right back on the couch where I started. You can find their books in local bookstores or on the web at JeffGalloway.com and JohnBingham.com.

The photo file preparation and cover graphic design were done by Olmsted Associates with the help of project manager Brian Sanderson. The final cover was designed by Andrew Ward, who has been creating the Crim poster and T-shirt art since 1992. Josh Visser did the typography and interior book design. Bobbie Christmas of Zebra Communications (www.zebraeditor.com) helped with editing, and rewrote some of the back cover copy. Color House Graphics printed the book and Sandy Rogers was especially helpful as the printing project manager.

Most of all, I would like to thank all the runners who sent me their stories. Thank you all for opening up your lives and giving us all the privilege of knowing your running "hearts and minds."

Anthony R. Ellis, M.D.
Crim Runner 2001 to present

THE STORY OF THE CRIM

Former speaker of the Michigan House Bobby Crim created The Bobby Crim 10 Mile Road Race for Special Olympics in 1977. He wanted to develop an event for the benefit of Michigan Special Olympics. Bobby began organizing a small road race in his home community to establish three main goals: first, to run a world-class road race in the city of Flint, Michigan; secondly, to raise charitable dollars for people with intellectual disabilities; and finally, to foster community pride and cooperation among the residents of the greater Flint area. Bobby received help from his administrative assistant, Lois Craig. She became the inaugural race director and a guiding light during her tenure at the helm from 1977 to 1993.

Five hundred and seventy-six brave souls participated in the inaugural running of the Crim ten-miler. The race originally started in front of Mott Community College and had to be moved twice as the race grew in popularity. The start was moved to its current downtown location on Saginaw Street in 1989.

The evolution of the Crim from its meager but ambitious beginnings to its current stature as the "Coolest Race In Michigan" has been dependent on the passion of many individuals. These include the Crim race directors and staff, and all the people who volunteer and support the Crim with their charity pledges. Many people donate their time and energy to help organize the challenging and fulfilling event year after year.

Bobby Crim's original idea has evolved to include something from each race director as well as input from runners and volunteers over time. The race has evolved just as cities and people change and grow with time.

Things inevitably move toward their fullest expression, and the Crim is no exception. Luckily, in the case of the Crim, the changes have been coincident with widespread community support and involvement.

The Crim has seen tremendous growth throughout the years. In 1985, the Crim Organization developed a Board of Directors, in addition to incorporating as a 501(c)(3) nonprofit corporation. The main goal of helping one charity, Michigan Special Olympics, expanded into assisting five others as well, including Big Brothers/Big Sisters of Greater Flint, Fair Winds Girl Scouts, Shelter of Flint, Genesee County Literacy Coalition, and the Crim Youth Development Program. The Crim has continued to support Special Olympics and in the year 2000, the Special Olympics Invitational was included in the Crim activities.

As time ticked on and the number of runners grew, so did the race options. Other distances soon joined the original ten-mile road race. In 1987, the 8K race was added. In 1988, the 5K Family Walk and Teddy Bear Trot became a part of the Crim tradition. With the new decade, the Crim 8K Walk, Friday's evening concert, and carnival rides were added. Saturday post-race entertainment rounded out the line up, and the Crim grew into a true family event.

The Bobby Crim Road Race continued to progress and expand, so the name was changed to represent the vast weekend of events it had become. In 1992, the name Crim Festival of Races was born and the event continued to grow. Since that time, the Crim Festival of Races has added the One-Mile Run, 8K Race-walk, Neighborhood Running Clubs, Crim Kids Classic, Crim Training Program, Beyond 2000 Program (community fitness program) and the Feelin' Good Mileage Club (school fitness program).

Running the Crim is akin to playing a round of golf during the Buick Open a couple of holes behind Tiger Woods. Like all races that have been around for a while, the Crim has its own mystique and charm. There are very few sports in which you can participate with world-class athletes such as Catherine Ndereba. Catherine competed in the Crim six consecutive years and won all six times. The people of Flint felt a special connection with Catherine when she won the silver medal in the 2004 Olympic marathon. The Crim attracts runners from all over the world, and in the 2004 Crim, participating athletes represented twenty countries.

In addition, the Crim brings out spectators along the racecourse, not only families and friends of the people running the course, but also many people who live along the course. Some are famous for having developed yearly rituals to welcome and motivate the runners. Nothing is quite like the feeling of running past a group of people who are looking at you with smiling faces and clapping, even though few of us run like the Kenyans.

The Crim course is unique and adds to the draw of the race. It has its own race lore and everyone who runs the Crim or is involved in the race knows of the challenging Bradley hills. Running down the bricks toward the finish line on Saginaw Street signals the end of effort and the beginning of celebration, at least until the next year. The course winds its way through old, worn-out industrial and manufacturing areas of Flint, Michigan, but also passes through some of the nicest neighborhoods Flint has to offer. The Crim is a part of the history of Flint, Michigan, and the racecourse provides a view into the soul of the city and its people.

The Crim Festival of Races contributed more than an estimated eight million dollars of financial support to the city during its race weekend in 2003. No other weekend during the year brings the downtown Flint area alive in quite the same way as Crim weekend. The Crim Festival of Races draws together all the diversity of Flint for a day of celebration of pure human endeavor. It is the triumph of determination over obstacles to help the less fortunate.

The Crim Training Program (CTP) is an extension of the race and provides other direct benefits to the city of Flint and its people. The Crim Training Program is the largest of its kind in the world. The number of participants shown in the table that follows demonstrates its growth and expanding impact.

The Crim Training Program provides running programs for local schools and helps create the next generation of runners who seek to preserve their health and add to their longevity. In the Crim Training Program, people go from sitting on the sidelines to active participants and frequently have a life-changing experience in the process. Many of the former Crim Training Program participants have become group leaders and carry on the tradition of helping people take control their health and well being through walking and running. What could be more helpful in a state with some challenging public health problems than a program that motivates people to take better care of their health and have fun at the same time?

Throughout its growth, the original visions of the Crim have not been lost or compromised. The Crim Festival of Races is ranked one of the top world-class races at its distance. The Crim has developed overwhelming community support. The Crim has contributed more than 1.2 million dollars to Special Olympics over the years. From volunteers to participants to spectators, Crim pride is visible across thousands of faces during the fourth weekend of August, year after year.

The Crim is something different to each participant and to all members of the Crim staff and volunteers who make it happen. How could you not care about something so fundamentally good? The Crim inspires people in the service of others. The people who love the Crim invite you to join us. We'll look for you in late August, on the course, on the sidelines, or behind the scenes. The runners' stories follow. Enjoy.

The Crim staff and Anthony R. Ellis, M.D.
June 2005

CRIM TEN-MILE TOTAL FINISHERS:

1977	576	1991	4,716
1978	1,197	1992	4,762
1979	1,992	1993	5,212
1980	1,992	1994	5,055
1981	2.915	1995	5,354
1982	4,036	1996	5,773
1983	5,037	1997	5,766
1984	4,600	1998	6,099
1985	4,779	1999	6,140
1986	4,698	2000	6,076
1987	3,543	2001	6,781
1988	3,211	2002	6,251
1989	3,876	2003	6,059
1990	4.437	2004	7,258

CRIM TRAINING PROGRAM (CTP) PARTICIPANTS

1995	130	2001	374
1996	225	2002	488
1997	271	2003	643
1998	327	2004	774
1999	217	2005	973
2000	250		

CHAPTER ONE
Inaugural Crimsters

RUNNING SCARED

RILEY MCLINCHA

Courtesy of Marathon Foto

AGE: 54
YEARS RUNNING: 29
CRIM FINISHES: ALL 28
YEARS IN CTP: 5
RESIDENCE: CLIO, MI
OCCUPATION: ENTERTAINER,
RETIRED GM TRADESMAN

There I stood in a herd of about six hundred runners on Horrigan Drive on the Mott Community College campus. I suddenly realized I was in way over my head. I looked around and saw *real* runners with *real* running shoes wearing singlets emblazoned with the names of track clubs. I looked down at my Kmart Trax and thought, "What the hell am I doing here? I can't run ten miles and keep up with these people." I had *never* run a race before. What was I thinking? I was so naïve about running that a month prior I was asking the owner of the Ski Haus to be my sponsor.

"The money goes to Special Olympics," I told him.

"Do you think you will win?" he asked me.

I shrugged and considered the question before giving my answer. "I don't know. Maybe."

It was close to noon, and I was in the throng of real runners at the start of the very first Bobby Crim Road Race. Before arriving at the starting line I sat alone in the shade of the Prahl Center of MCC trying to get some relief from the ninety-five-degree heat and the humidity that was also in the nineties. I looked for a familiar face among the hundreds of runners moving to and from Ballenger Field House where race numbers were being picked up. I did not recognize a soul. Why should I? None of my friends ran, and I had only recently begun to run out of fear.

A few months earlier, March 5, 1977, to be exact, I came home from work. My wife yelled to me as I was getting out of the van. "Go to the hospital! Your mom has taken a turn for the worse."

She had been admitted a week earlier with heart problems. I arrived at the hospital as fast as I could and walked to her room. It was empty. I found a nurse who took me to find my mother.

"Has the doctor talked to you?" she asked before opening the door.

"No. Why?" I answered.

"Oh you better wait here, then," was all she said.

When the doctor arrived he told me my mom had a massive heart attack and that she was dead. I went numb. The doctor continued talking but I never heard a word he was saying.

She was only fifty-three, the same age I am as I write this. Way too young. In the weeks that followed her death my mind kept comparing her age to mine. I was more than twenty-six years old and haunted by the idea that "My life is half over if I die at her age." She had been overweight and hadn't exercised at all. I was scared, and I told myself I wouldn't end up that way, but like most Americans I just couldn't get into exercising regularly. Fortunately for me, that soon changed.

In June I heard there was to be a ten-mile road race later that summer and anyone could run. The gossip was that joggers like me could run with famous runners like Bill Rodgers. "Who's he?" I wondered. Little did I know in a year's time he would replace Al Kaline as my favorite sports figure.

Ten miles was five times farther than I'd ever

jogged, but I made it a goal to be at the starting line on August 27. I did not know anything about training or know anyone to ask. Unlike today there were no running stores in the area where I could go for expertise, so I made up my own two-step program. First, see if you can run the distance. I went to Hamady High School track and ran as slow as I possibly could, for ten miles! Second, I waited a week to ten days for my legs to stop screaming, "You stupid ass, don't ever do that again." I would then ignore their pleas and repeat the ten miles with a slight increase in speed. It was hard to psych myself up after each run, as running was never something I liked doing, but at least after the first time, I knew the distance was do-able and left the track for the open roads.

When the race application came out, it stated the contact person was some guy named John Gault. I called him for course directions and wrote them down. One week before the race I ran the course and was stumped and amazed at the improvement in my time. One week to recover, then I would run the real thing, The Bobby Crim Road Race for Special Olympics.

I stood up slowly and moved from the shade of the Prahl Center into the hottest and muggiest noon I remember to this day. Walking to the starting line I could not get over the feeling of being alone, although I was among hundreds of people. At the starting line I met a married couple.

"Is this your first race?" the husband asked me.

"Yes," I told them "How did you know?"

"You look scared," the wife answered.

I think they were being kind. My Kmart shoes, my Three Stooges tank top, and high school gym trunks left over from the '60s were probably the real giveaway. The couple gave me some advice (about racing, not my clothing). "Go slow," they said, and take all the water that's available. The gun went off, and I never saw them again, ever. I still remember their last name and that they were from Lapeer. I had met my first runners, and they made me feel better. What wonderful people, I thought. They were much like the thousands of runners I would meet in decades to come.

The throng of runners snaked down Horrigan Drive to Court Street then straight downtown to Harrison. The heat did not seem to be a problem to anyone. I felt pretty good when we turned onto Third Avenue and past the two-mile mark at the old Durant Hotel. A mile later at GMI (now Kettering University), I felt I was slowing a little but kept plugging along. Water stations were not as plentiful as in today's Crim races, and no one carried water with them. Thank goodness the heat did bring out a few spectators with hoses. Through Mott Park and the Bradley hills I soaked myself whenever possible. By the time I turned on Chicago Avenue and headed toward the six-mile mark, my body temperature was approaching the temperature inside my shoes.

Immediately after crossing Miller Road, I was hit with a bombshell. The course turned onto Hawthorne. When I had run the course in training, I had gone straight to Parkside, cutting off nearly a mile of the course. I suddenly became aware of the reason why my time the week before had been so good. My heart sank. It was then that I started walking. I didn't know we were allowed to walk, but seeing others doing it, I gave in and copied my new brethren. On Hawthorne I watched as people in their yards drank beer and shook their heads at us. I could see their point and wanted to go and join them, despite never having drunk a beer before. Anything would have tasted like ambrosia at that point. Somehow I fought off the temptation. I had started something and had to finish it.

I "Galloway-ed" the last few miles, though this was years before anyone would hear of the Galloway Method. Near the nine-mile mark a hose hung from a stepladder. I stood beneath it and drenched myself. The weight of my shoes afterwards slowed me down even more. There were no breathable mesh uppers back then, just padded leather.

Hitting the bricks and crossing the finish line was anticlimactic because I just wanted the race to be over. My time was about 94 minutes, and I was 411 out of 576 finishers.

My family found me immediately, and the first thing

out of my mouth was, "I will never...ever do that again."

I made it to the sidewalk, sat down, and took off my saturated Trax shoes, which must have weighed six pounds apiece. The cheap insoles were made of cardboard and had disintegrated into pulp. As I sat feeling bad about the loss of my shoes, the last few runners came in. A cheer went up for a haggard old man wearing of all things white dress shoes with platform heels. I was witnessing the birth of a Crim legend, Ed Wiberg. I threw *my* shoes in a trash-can and walked barefoot, a Crim unknown, but a hero to family members at my side. They looked at me like I was nuts and had lost my memory, when I said, "I can't wait until next year."

Riley has run every Crim race since 1977. He has been a Crim training group leader for five years. You may also know him as the guy who runs while "drubbling" three basketballs. He has been on Ripley's Believe It or Not and The Today Show. He also won a Trivial Pursuit question contest with his question about drubbling. He was instrumental in getting several of the submissions for this collection. Thanks Riley!

LITTLE DIFFERENCES MAKE A BIG DIFFERENCE

DAN MIGLIN

AGE: 50
YEARS RUNNING: 29
CRIM FINISHES: ALL 28
RESIDENCE: GOODLETTSVILLE, TN
OCCUPATION: UAW TEAM LEADER,
    SATURN

There isn't anything remarkable about this story; it could be told by countless others. This story is not about what's been done in the Crim. It's about what one can become because of the Crim. It's about realizing that it's the "little difference that makes a big difference" in life's successes. Over the years, the Crim has helped me develop the skills needed to be successful in all areas of life. I've learned how to overcome obstacles, be persistent, and realize that being a small part of something can add up to something much greater.

We all have obstacles we face in life, and we all have handicaps that may be seen or unseen. The little difference is our handicaps and the big difference is whether they stop us from succeeding. You don't have to look far among the Crim participants to be inspired by people like Ed Wiberg. There are also blind runners, wheelers, and Special Olympics athletes who challenge themselves and inspire others in the process.

In my first Crim, I ran against my brother Frank. He is five years older than I am, and he is an ex-Marine. I don't recall ever beating him at anything, and I didn't that day. He beat me by twelve runners. To this day, running in that first Crim is the most physical thing that I've ever done in my life. In the years to follow my persistence paid off, and I was able to best my brother on several occasions.

The Crim memories are long lasting and unique. Whether you run, volunteer, organize, cheer, or donate, you become a piece of an extraordinary puzzle.

Over the years, I've raised between twenty-five dollars and $500 a year for Special Olympics. I've watched dollars turn into hundreds, hundreds turn into thousands, and thousands turn into millions. Little differences can make a big difference. It's a little difference to think about being a part of the Crim. It makes a big difference when you become a part of the Crim.

The first time I met Riley was in a Dale Carnegie class. We both told a story about our first Crim race. I've run all twenty-eight since then. Riley passed on an email to me about this book. I've never considered myself much of a writer. I guess the point I'm trying to make is this: You don't have to be a superstar to be successful. The little things that we do in life add up to make a big impact.

Rewards come from being a part of something gratifying like the Crim. I haven't been the fastest runner or the slowest runner, but I've still gotten rewards for being a runner in the Crim. I've been humbled by men, women, and children. Everyone who passes me or that I pass is living his or her own Crim story. Their little difference makes a big difference.

Dan enjoys his job at the Saturn Corporation in Spring Hill, Tennessee. Over the last eleven years he has organized a group of runners from Michigan and Tennessee in the corporate division. He feels fortunate to be one of the few Crim runners that has finished every ten-mile from 1977 to the present. As you will see, in addition to motivation, diligence, and fortitude, it takes a bit of luck to finish a race like the Crim every year. Dan has two sons, Jason and Logan, who look forward to the Crim Festival of Races each August. They have a goal to run together in the thirtieth Crim ten-mile race.

GIVING SOMETHING BACK

MARK BAUMAN

Courtesy of brightroom

AGE: 55
YEARS RUNNING: 39
CRIM FINISHES: ALL 28
YEARS IN CTP: SINCE INCEPTION
RESIDENCE: FLUSHING, MI
OCCUPATION: OWNER/OPERATOR BAUMAN'S
  RUNNING AND WALKING SHOP

Running is my hobby, livelihood and a way for me to help others. Some may wonder why I've run in every Crim race from the inaugural race to the present. The reason is plain and simple: I love running. I've been running since 1966 and competed for Mott Junior College and later for Murray State. Since I started, Mott and the Crim have changed their names slightly, but running the Crim every year is still a thrill, even after twenty-eight years although not in quite the same way it was when I tried to run it fast.

Last year several of us ran the race with squirt guns. We had a ball with the kids on the course. It was no big deal to stop and fill our shooters every mile or so. We were just having fun and enjoying the day. The finish line seemed to come too soon.

I briefly took a teaching job in Seminole, Florida, but soon came back to Michigan. It's been quite a while since I sold running shoes out of the back of my car. In 1978 I turned my garage into a running store and joined the few lucky folks who can practice a hobby and earn a living with it too. Running, and helping others to enjoy and excel at it, has given me back as much as I put in, and more. I have enjoyed being a part of the country's first running boom. Being involved in the running scene in Flint was part of the reason I came back to Michigan after living in Florida.

Another enjoyable aspect of running in Flint is the relationships I've developed with the people I've met and trained with. Many of them are faster than I am, but they treat other runners, including me, as though we are important to them despite our differing abilities.

I also enjoy the stories we tell each other on training runs, some of which are even true. Where else can one find a group of friends who will think it's normal to run in sub-zero temperatures in the winter and in ninety-degree heat in the summer?

My involvement in the local running club, the Riverbend Striders, was a natural extension of my interest in running. When I moved back to Flint from Florida, John Gault was organizing and managing local road races on his own. People were looking for races that weren't sixty to one hundred miles away. John and I put together some races and before long, we had several. We added a group of winter and summer runs and added walking events.

As time went on, John and Anne married and developed a business managing races. They wanted to put on the best events in the area and increase the choices for local runners. They later went on to manage the largest number of races in the state. It has been a pleasure to work with them over the years. The help we get from the other members of the Striders is overwhelming and gratifying. The local runners are always thanking us for putting on the events that allow them to get out and do their thing.

The Crim Training Program has always been special to me, too. From day one, I have gotten a thrill from helping novice runners advance to longer running distances and meet their goals. To see the sense of accomplishment on the faces of the new runners as they finish four, then five, and eventually ten miles, is something I'll never grow tired of. It has been a long time for me since my first time running, and I have forgotten how it feels to have a seemingly impossible goal become possible. I love to see it in the faces of the training program participants, though. I enjoy their smiles of achievement when they talk about the Crim and how they felt coming down the bricks on Saginaw Street.

Even though I have running streaks in the Boston Marathon, Detroit Marathon, and other races, the Crim is my favorite. The Crim attracts some of the fastest runners in the world, and I get to line up on the same starting line as they do at 8:00 a.m. on the fourth Saturday in August in Flint, Michigan. For me, the Crim is Flint and vice versa. Not running the Crim would be like being a Piston fan and never going to a game. It is my hometown race and the people who organize it, the runners, and the people along the course, all have a permanent place in my heart.

Mark and his wife Joan have been married for eleven years. They have three children named Jeff, Brent, and Sonya. Mark and Joan are the caring, involved grandparents of six grandchildren. The grandchildren are: Brenden, Lauren, Madison, Evan, Olivia, and Lucas. The proud and happy grandparents have taken to their role with passion and enthusiasm.

I met Mark while I was preparing for my first Crim. He sold me my first pair of real running shoes. I picked a name brand that runs a lot of popular ads on television, but Mark tried to get me to broaden my horizons a bit. Mark is selfless and won't blow his own horn, but I will blow his for him. He has run the Boston Marathon thirty-six times in a row since 1970. This is the fourth longest streak among active runners at Boston. He has run all the Crim ten-milers and all the Detroit Free Press marathons. He has completed more than 100 marathons, with a personal best in the low 2:30's. Despite all of his successes his head is of normal size, which is almost as amazing as his number of consecutive races.

CHAPTER TWO
Running Inspirations

Shirts

BRIAN BARKEY

Courtesy of Marathon Foto

BRIAN

AGE: 60
YEARS RUNNING: 30+
CRIM FINISHES: 22
YEARS IN CTP: 9
RESIDENCE: FLINT, MI
OCCUPATION: ATTORNEY

It doesn't take long running footraces before you accumulate two tangible exhibits to your new avocation: race numbers and T-shirts. The race numbers I have tacked to a bulletin board in my kitchen. I've had to rearrange them twice to make room for more. The shirts are another story, this story.

I have favorites. One, from the Trenton Treadmill Run, has a heart on it that glows in the dark. One from a race in Frankenmuth has *lederhosen* painted on it. I have shirts from prestigious runs like the Crim that I wear when traveling, because they nearly always attract a comment from another runner. There are ugly shirts, too, that I wear as a runner's inside joke.

I gave them to my kids when they were home, but now that they have gone, I have too many shirts to use by myself. Who, after all, buys a dozen T-shirts a year? I keep out the ones from memorable runs (the 1992 Dexter to Ann Arbor half-marathon where a train crossed the course during the race, for example) and the rest, never worn, go into boxes.

I wear one shirt with pride every week, though I did not run a race to get it. It is the shirt that identifies me as a Crim Training Program group leader. In fifteen weeks, this program prepares novice runners and those who have never put on a pair of running shoes for the hilly ten-mile Crim road race. Nearly 600 participants in the ten-mile program are divided into groups of fifteen to twenty and assigned two group leaders. The leaders guide the group, incrementally, to greater and greater distances leading up to the event. The program also provides nutrition and injury-prevention lectures. I have been a group leader for nine of the ten years the program has been in existence, and it has recharged my enthusiasm like nothing else in my twenty-nine years of running.

Before long I realized that every first-time training participant has a reason why they have joined the training program. The participant has quit smoking, for example, and wants to do something as physically good for them as smoking was bad. The participant is marking a significant mid-life recalibration; they've had a change in jobs, marital status, or their children have left home. Many are trying to recapture the energy of younger days. Some seek the youthful energy they lost or never had. During these weekly group runs, I frequently get to hear their stories, and everyone has a story about why they joined the program.

I had not yet heard Shirin's story when I saw her on race morning. She walked and ran with the others in her training group until she reached the halfway point in the race, where the course takes the runners up the first of three steep hills. People who run this race know and respect the Bradley hills. The people in the adjacent apartment complex come out to cheer on the runners and always provide sorely needed motivation. I was alarmed to see that Shirin was crying. I recognized her as being in the training program and I was worried that, with half the race left, she would have a hard time.

When I asked her about it, she said she was actually feeling fresh, but that running past the apartment complex at the start of the Bradley hills always made her sad.

It was where her son had lived. Her son, she explained, was the reason she had joined the training program.

While he was a student at Kettering University, his fraternity had always volunteered at a water station during the race. The runners' enthusiasm had always interested him, and when he graduated from college, he decided to run the Crim instead of standing on the sidelines.

During the training, he struggled more than he should have. A visit to the doctor produced alarming news. He was diagnosed with a rare form of cancer. He unfortunately lost his battle with cancer two years later. He was never able to run the race he always intended to run. Shirin was running his race for him.

Another group leader and I decided we would join her. As word spread among the people we saw from the training program, more joined us. When we turned the corner onto Saginaw Street to run the final quarter mile down the bricks to the finish line, we were nearly twenty people strong. As we passed under the timing clock, hand in hand, Shirin looked up and called out her son's name. While runners around us were untying the Champion Chips from their running shoes, we were holding each other in tears. I still get gooseflesh every time I tell this story.

Life is unbelievably large and can seem arbitrary, sometimes. How nice it is to discover that we are in a bigger race with people who are more like us than different. Being a group leader has taught me that each of us has a story. If I listen hard for these stories, I can hear them. It's a privilege to be present every summer when it happens. I hope to wear my Crim Training Program group leader shirt, with pride, for a long, long time.

Brian is a fixture at the Crim Training Program and is famous on the Crim running scene. He is a local attorney, and rumor has it he met his wife, Dorie, while she was in the training group he was leading. Brian and Dorie are fortunate in that they share a passion for running. Brian's self-deprecating sense of humor and dedication to the Crim are singularly unique. He took our fledgling group of novice run-

ners through a half-marathon training program for eight weeks on his own time in the spring of 2002. He is one of the most positive people I have ever met.

A Penguin in Florida

LENKE KRATOCHVIL

AGE: 55
YEARS RUNNING: 1
CRIM FINISHES: 1
RESIDENCE: London, Ontario
OCCUPATION: Architectural Drafting
    Technician/Interior Design Consultant

I experienced an incredible feeling as we drove over sparkling blue waters as far as my eyes could see. Seven Mile Bridge, like a ribbon in the breeze, unfurled its lazy path toward Key West. With the windows down and sunroof open, we stopped at a red light on Marathon Key, when an ad caught my eye. There would be a running event across the bridge that weekend. We were willing to abandon our existing plans to watch the runners. Unfortunately, our flight back home was inflexible, so my husband and I left our idle thoughts and the warm weather behind.

Back home, after all the snow disappeared, my husband enrolled in a Learn to Run Clinic and started losing a noticeable amount of weight. He was well into training for a 10K run, when I finally decided to tag along one night to see what all the hype was about. I knew I could never run, so I tried the walking clinic, which happened to be on the same night.

I was not new to walking. My longest and most demanding hike was down to the bottom of the Grand

Canyon and back up the same day. Although that trip was a few years back, I did not find the walking clinic challenging enough at first. The distances were quite short. It was almost not worth my while to go there to walk around the block a few times. I could do that amount of walking at home without getting into the car. Nevertheless, I met some great people in the group, so I decided to stick with it. Later came the hill training, and with it, the challenge.

At the end of the clinic, I enthusiastically entered my first race, but it turned out to be disappointing. The organizers forgot about our small group of 10K walkers, aware of only those walking the 5K. There was confusion as to where they would place us at the start, but the finish was even more of a letdown. As we were walking our second lap, some of the volunteers were already packing up and going home. I began to regret signing up for the half-marathon clinic.

One day during a clinic, a race-walker joined us in the park and upon hearing about my first race, suggested that I try the Crim. It would be fun, definitely had more participants, I would see the canyons, and they served beer during the race. I wasn't quite sure what to make of the Crim, but it certainly sounded like it could be fun. Because my training happened to call for a distance of 18K the weekend of the Crim, I signed up with my husband for the ten-mile run. I figured that distance was close enough. What else could I do? I couldn't get him or anyone else interested in the 8K walk.

The difference didn't seem all that ridiculous at the time. After all, my husband's half-marathon training was identical to mine. We did the same hills and distances. On a few nights when I was the only walker who showed up for the clinic, I tried running with his group. It wasn't horrible; they just finished before I did.

When we arrived at the Sports and Fitness Expo, my husband was quite surprised that I ever suggested doing the Crim, and so was I. The experience was becoming increasingly intimidating for me as we mingled with thousands of athletes. Shopping always seems to cure my anxiety, so I indulged a little. As I spent far too long in the women's athletic wear section looking for running clothes, my husband left me there to hear John Bingham's presentation.

When I drifted out the door of the Expo with all my bags, the talk was already in progress. I wasn't particularly interested, but John "The Penguin" Bingham's down-to-earth running stories immediately captured my attention. I couldn't believe my ears. He was saying that it was not the end of the world to be slow, and offered the most amusing and unexpectedly funny ways to cope with being near the back of the pack. Coming in "dead last" was my greatest fear of the Crim.

The next morning we took our position near the back of the starting line and felt great about it. I was energized by all the excitement. Early in the race, I decided to pass an older gentleman, but he soon did the same to me, so I had to pass him again. By the time the race was over, I learned that he had just celebrated his seventy-fifth birthday and had run twenty-nine marathons. He never ran until he was fifty-three. Hmm! Penguins were friendly, just like John Bingham had described them.

I had the pleasure of meeting two other runners. Both had attended the Crim Training Program and knew the course, so they kept me informed of what was ahead. Thanks to them, I knew exactly when to start looking for the pink house at the four-mile marker. Strangely enough though, when I asked, neither of them knew about the canyons that I had come to see.

Stepping on the blue nine-mile marker was such an inspirational achievement for me, and it was great to share it with the two runners from Flint. With only half a mile to go, one picked up the pace and challenged us to do the same. We tried, but our burst of enthusiasm lasted just a short while. I didn't have much left in me. Instead, we opted to lag behind and save our energy for the very end. On the Saginaw Street bricks, my husband popped out of the crowd yelling and cheering, so we ran flat out to the end, gave our best mug to the camera, and stepped on the finish line together. Much to my amazement, hundreds of people were with us. We didn't finish dead last! It was so much fun.

Far too often we impose limits on our opportunities by not wanting to venture outside our comfort zone. I admit that if I had known that the Kenyans were running the same event, I would never have registered, but ignorance is bliss. I really thought I was going to see the canyons, not the Kenyans. As it turned out, I didn't see them, anyway, except on TV. What I did see were thousands of people having a great time. After the race I had just enough energy to hobble back to the Expo to get my "penguin" socks. They match my black-and-white running outfit, and they'll look great when I run the Seven Mile Bridge in Florida. Seven miles doesn't seem terribly long any more!

Lenke is an Architectural Drafting Technician whose background is in accounting and design. She worked for a variety of architectural, consulting and engineering firms for twenty years before recently becoming an interior design consultant. Since her first ten-mile Crim experience last year, she has successfully completed three half-marathons, choosing the Canyonlands Half-Marathon in Moab, Utah, to see the magnificent red cliff canyons. Although the Crim has no such geographical feature, Lenke feels it is still the most fun of the season. She will be returning again in 2005 with her husband and several members of her running/walking club, The London Pacers. This fall she will compete in the 20th Anniversary Budapest International Marathon and earn a finisher's medal from the city where she was born.

ATHLETE IN PROGRESS

SHARI ELLIS

Courtesy of brightroom

AGE: 39
YEARS RUNNING: 5
CRIM FINISHES: 4
YEARS IN CTP: 4
RESIDENCE: FLUSHING, MI
OCCUPATION: ASSISTANT DIRECTOR
ALPHA MONTESSORI SCHOOL

It has taken a long time to put my thoughts into words. This piece is simply about the ways in which the Crim and the Crim Training Program changed my life. My story is not about any exciting or dramatic events. In fact, it is not unusual for people who run this race, to have it change them. The change in my life has been subtle, yet profound. For you to understand the magnitude of what this race means to me, you must first see where I came from. Allow me to set the scene:

All of my life, since I was a little girl, I was very shy. In fact, I would say painfully shy. I was extremely quiet and my interests consisted mainly of reading and blending into the background. I never drew attention to myself in any way, shape, or form. At times, I deliberately took the long way to my next class, even if it meant being tardy, to avoid the hallway where the boys sat along the benches and watched the girls go by. Some of my peers believed me to be stuck up or stand-offish, which was so ridiculous, because it was totally not the case.

I was the kind of adolescent who was not exactly overweight, but not what you would consider thin either. I was also every gym teacher's worst nightmare. I was not athletic by any stretch of the imagination. I hated gym class, and I especially hated running with a passion. Gym class was my nemesis all my school life. I was the first kid out when playing dodge ball, the last kid picked for every team. Even the fat kids were chosen before me; that really hurt. Of course, I was always the last one around the track. I had side stitches, I couldn't breathe, and I always came in last place, feeling defeated and humiliated by the end of each gym class.

If you were to ask me prior to 2001, I would have bet you *any* money that I would never ever run, unless someone big was chasing me. By now, you're probably wondering what this story is doing in this book, and how it could possibly have a happy ending that involves the word "running." Believe me, I know, the answer is still shocking to me as well. This is how it happened:

Fast forward to my adulthood. I am someone who exercises, but not consistently. I am not really overweight, but not in great shape, either. As I get older, I see my weight fluctuate and proportion itself differently on my body from year to year. I find myself wearing my fat clothes more than my skinny clothes as the years go by.

When I was thirty-five years old and my second child was about nine months old, I saw a Crim Training Program brochure on my desk at work. I can't explain it, except to say that I was captivated by what I read. The brochure said that if I was someone who exercised or ran within the past year, that I could train for and run/walk the ten-mile road race. I couldn't believe it. I thought I could walk forever, and the running? Well, I could run a little, as long as I had walk breaks, which were promised in the brochure. The deadline to register was in four days. It was now or never; I had to make a decision fast. I felt like it was my big opportunity to really get in shape. After all, I wasn't getting any younger. If I could finish the ten-mile road race I would really be stepping out of my box. I had never in my life even dreamed that I could possibly accomplish something of that magnitude, yet, I really felt like it was possible, because of the program description of running and walking.

My mind was made up; I had to find a partner. None of my friends would have anything to do with it, so I reluctantly asked my husband. The reason that I was reluctant was not that he was undesirable as a running partner, but because I thought we wouldn't be in the same group because he would be a better runner than me. However, I soon learned that neither one of us could run to the corner. The playing field was more level than I had thought, so we signed up.

I will never forget that first year in the training program. The first meeting at the Hurley Health and Fitness Center blew me away. I heard Brian Barkey describe every mile of the Crim, all the while reassuring the newcomers that we, too, would experience the glory of this race. I couldn't breathe. I was spellbound, and I wanted badly to succeed. I was committed to doing the ten-mile road race, whatever it took.

The following week we were put in our training groups and I looked around at all the new faces and thought "These people will not be my friends. How is this going to work?"

Much to my surprise and delight, I *loved* my running group. I was astonished at how many wonderful people I met that first summer and how many of them continue to be my great friends. I looked forward to every Tuesday night run. It was actually more fun than I could have imagined. Even when it was really hard, I loved it. I followed the fifteen week training calendar religiously, and I ran/walked my first Crim in 2001. I fell in love with the race and the people I met along the way. I couldn't bear the thought of it all being over after the Crim. Many of my new friends from the training program along with my husband and me, continued to run and walk through the winter that first year and every year since that 2001 training season.

I am approaching my fortieth birthday, and I will tell you what the Crim has given me. Since that first year, I have gained a new sense of confidence in myself and my body. I have for the first time in my whole life maintained a body weight and size that I feel pretty good about. No more fat and skinny clothes, just clothes that consistently fit me. I now feel like anything is possible. If someone like me can participate in the Crim every year, what else can I do? People think of me as an athlete now and assume that I must have always been one. I love this! I encourage them to tell me all about what they think I was like in high school. I hear things like, "I picture you as a cheerleader or a volleyball star or maybe a soccer player." It makes me laugh and feel great. I always set them straight, eventually, but I do enjoy the mistake.

I also attended my twenty year high school class reunion in 2003. Mind you, I never would have gone to the reunion, had it not been for the confidence I achieved from running the Crim. I did not announce my new running affinity, or reveal running as my secret for looking better twenty years later than I did in high school. I didn't have to. The fact that I was there, and I knew that I looked and felt great, and my thighs didn't touch each other was enough to make me feel like a million dollars.

The Crim also gave me an incredible experience during my last pregnancy. I ran throughout my third pregnancy, including the Crim ten-mile race when I was thirty-four weeks pregnant. I could not and would not have ever done that, had it not been for my confidence in myself and my body and the love and support of the people involved with the Crim Training Program. As a thirty-nine-year year old mother of three, I found that running also helped me get back into shape after the birth of my third child, much faster and easier than with my previous pregnancies.

I hope by now that you can see what a huge impact the Crim and the training program have had on my life. You may wonder why, after I gained the initial benefits of running and walking, I continue to join the program and run the Crim every year. After all, I could just as easily have learned what I needed to learn and never run the race again, but that's not possible for me. It's hard to imagine not running now. The Crim, the training program, and the running community in Flint have become a big part of my life and the life of my family.

The friends I've made while training and running are very dear to me. They are all very special people, and we care about each other. We celebrate birthdays together. We are each others cheerleaders and support group. If I know that my running group is expecting me to run, I will definitely show up, even if I don't really feel like it. After the run, I always feel better; partly because of the run and partly because I just spent an hour or two with great friends. We struggle together and we are all the better for the effort.

That all this came from a flyer lying on my desk is hard to figure out. Perhaps I was meant to be a runner. Maybe there was a shy athlete inside of me all along, waiting for the right circumstances to go out for a little run.

Shari is a 1983 graduate of Linden High School. She obtained a Bachelor's degree in Charleston, S.C., then a Masters Degree in Social Work from Michigan State University. Shari has been happily married for twelve years. She is the loving mother of three beautiful daughters, Alaina, Serena, and Mia. Shari has been working at Alpha Montessori School in downtown Flint for five years and loves her job. Since her first Crim ten-mile race in 2001, she has gone on to run five half-marathons and is toying with the idea of running the Detroit Free Press Marathon this fall. Shari loves the Crim and wouldn't dream of missing it unless injury or death occurred.

A Mere 28 Hours

MIKE LAUX

AGE: 49
YEARS RUNNING: 22
CRIM FINISHES: 21
RESIDENCE: FLUSHING, MI
OCCUPATION: ACCOUNTANT

I am a runner. A Crim runner. Like all of us I have many roles in life. When I think of the things that define me, being a Crim runner is definitely one of them. It began with the 1984 race, twenty-one years ago. No, it actually began while I was watching the 1983 race. A coworker had run that year, and my wife Kathy and I had attended. I had great admiration for my friend's accomplishment. A few days after the race, I proudly announced to Kathy that I was going to run the race the next year and that I would begin training in the spring.

Unimpressed, she challenged, "If you're serious, you'll start training right now!"

So I did. I trained for a week or two in canvas tennis shoes, then with my first pair of real running shoes. A few months later, I entered my first race, followed by a dozen more that first year. I know it was a dozen, because I wrote them all down. As an accountant, I'm into recording things. I've recorded every mile for twenty-one years.

A group of guys from work all set their sights on the 1984 Crim. Two of them stand out. One inspired me the first year, and the second has inspired me ever since. Sam Reid, a smoker who was tall and somewhat overweight surprised me that first year with the challenge of a $25 bet and a claim that he would beat me. Sam, to his credit, did finish that race. I still have a copy of his $25 check to Special Olympics and his handwritten note proclaiming me as "an example for all persons who set goals and achieve them."

Then there is Paul Riker. I don't remember too much about us that first year, but I can't forget the years that have followed. The 1984 race was the first for Paul as well. He, too, has run every one since. He ran the year he had angioplasty in the spring. During the four years he was on international assignment in Japan, he returned each August to run the Crim. He is a true Crim runner and my good friend.

We still run our long runs together each summer and meet at 7:00 a.m. each fourth Saturday in August at the clock. We have a pre-race ritual (some things are private) and start each race together. About eighty to ninety minutes later, we meet up again to reflect, celebrate, and eat pizza!

When I started, it was called the "Bobby Crim Road Race for Special Olympics." While the focus for some has shifted, for me Special Olympics will always be another good reason to run. I'm greatly indebted to all the loyal people who have pledged and supported me in this cause these last two decades. Special thanks go to Jim Walroth, who alone has contributed more than $1,000 over the years.

I can't honestly say that I've had to overcome great obstacles to run, but there was one year early on when Kathy's sister got married at 11:00 on race day. Fortunately, I was a bit faster then, and she had the good sense to have the wedding at First Presbyterian Church, right on Saginaw Street. By the way, I did shower and actually made it with about five minutes to spare. The three years I was in night school, training was a bit harder, but for the most part, I've been blessed with good health and good luck.

Countless people have encouraged me during the years. Kathy has been the best coach any wife could be, after her initial challenge. My eight-year-old nephew Matt ran the one-mile with me in 1994 and flew in from out of state to do his first full Crim this year in sixty-three minutes! Many other family members who have come to watch the race have always been supportive. Ray Ploucha cheered at the four-mile mark. Don and Bob's encouragement pushed me forward at the Bradley hills. I could always count on the Plumbs near the nine-mile marker, Jim and Sharon Pelc on Saginaw Street, and Ron Gregory's post-race notes.

In the end, though, running the Crim isn't something you do for other people. It certainly isn't something you do for glory. There isn't an age group old enough for me to ever win! It's hard to explain the joy, satisfaction, and sense of well being it brings. I just know it does.

It's about much more than just the race itself. It's wonderful to be active and get involved in the day Flint comes alive. Twenty-one Crims at an average time of eighty minutes is a mere twenty-eight hours. Over a lifetime of nearly fifty years, maybe that isn't much. It feels like a lot when I reflect on it, and I'm proud and lucky to have had the chance to run. Not everyone gets that chance.

As Sam wrote, it's about "setting goals and achieving them." It's about long training runs on hot summer mornings. It's about T-shirts. It's about lifelong friendships. It's about defining yourself. I am a runner. A Crim runner.

Mike lives in Flushing with his wife Kathy of twenty-three years. Kathy has been Mike's running coach for twenty-two of those years. When he is not running, Mike works as an accountant for GM Service Parts Operations. Outside of work, Mike and Kathy enjoy traveling and generally having fun together as a couple. Mike dedicated his Crim story to his running partner Paul Riker who has been with him on the roads and at the races for twenty-two years.

A Special Crim Medal

SKIP UEBELHART

AGE: 56
YEARS RUNNING: 6
CRIM FINISHES: 5
YEARS IN CTP: 1
RESIDENCE: FLINT, MI
OCCUPATION: RETIRED
PHYSICIAN

My brief career in running has been driven by the thrill of competition. I trained to run fast, and I trained to race. Achievement and joy were dictated by awards and new personal records. The pure joy of running had eluded me. The fun of running for its own sake, that freedom of movement with a breeze caressing my face and the "high" that so many runners talk about just wasn't there for me.

I was training once again for the 8K Crim run, when Lori, my twenty-four-year old daughter, announced she would attempt the ten-mile race. She had run several 5K races in other Crim festivals, but had never gone ten miles. Perhaps she was motivated as a bystander at the famous marathon near her home in Boston.

A determined person, her training was geared toward building up distance and endurance. Suddenly, my own goal changed. Here was a chance to run with my daughter, side by side. It would be special to share the prestigious Crim experience with her. For one race, I would forget the speed. I would leave the worry about "placing" at home. I could run just for the fun of running.

Admittedly, the early morning rain on Crim day dampened our enthusiasm. Once the race started and the weather improved, our spirits lifted. Immersed in a running mass of humanity, we began to feel the sheer electricity of the event. We felt all the fun and excitement the Crim had to offer. For the first time during a race, I took the time to look around me. I watched people talking and laughing, runners bonding, and families sharing the special day together. I felt the rush of cheers and saw thousands of festive bystanders. There were "high fives," the spray of water in our faces, and the crowd encouragement to keep us going.

We felt the fun the revelers at Cashew corner were having, relished the music from Sweet Adelaide's, and stepped to the beat of "When the Saints Come Marching In." The senior citizens along the Bradley hills pot and pan brigade were enjoying the race as much as any of the runners. Their smiles helped us up and over the hills.

The adrenaline rush from all the excitement, the cheers, and the entertainment gave us the determination and strength to carry on. In her first ever ten-mile run, Lori never lost a step. Finally came the red bricks, and with one final sprint, we surged across the finish line. I gave Lori a hearty hug and well-deserved congratulations. For her, this year's Crim represented a personal distance record. For me, the thrill was in sharing the experience with my daughter.

We celebrated Lori's twenty-fifth birthday on the day following the Crim. I gave her one additional gift. Slowly, she removed the ribbon and wrapping from the small package. She removed the tissue paper and uncovered my Crim medal. Decades from now, when I am but a memory, I want Lori to remove these Crim medals from the back of her drawer and share the story with her children and grandchildren. I want her to remember with a smile the fun and love we shared long ago at the Crim.

After Skip retired from his medical practice, he was fortunate to discover a new challenging avocation. Running has become a "fountain of youth" for Skip and an activity that the whole family can share. Across time, Skip hopes the Crim will be a stepping stone toward his ultimate running goal, the Boston Marathon.

CRIM FACT:
Eight ambulances and 200 medical personnel are on call throughout the Crim course.

From Couch Potatoes to Crimsters

ANTHONY ELLIS

AGE: 41
YEARS RUNNING: 5
CRIM FINISHES: 4
YEARS IN CTP: 4
RESIDENCE: FLUSHING, MI
OCCUPATION: GERIATRIC PSYCHIATRIST

During the summer of 2000, my wife Shari asked me to go to a fitness expo in downtown Flint, Michigan. She has always been in charge of family health, fitness, and diet, which is a good thing, because I count chips and dip as a vegetable. She keeps track of the vitamins, flax seed oil, and granola bars and won't let me buy white bread, whole milk, or sugary cereals. The expo turned out to be for the Crim Festival of Races. We had never heard of or paid any attention to the Crim and knew nothing of the local running subculture.

The Crim races were to be held the next morning. The tension and excitement at the expo were palpable. There were elite runners from Kenya and hundreds of would-be runners from all walks of life. Shari coerced me into signing up for one of the Crim events with her. We settled on the 8K walk, not knowing what the heck a kilometer was. The decision was based partly on our newborn daughter's involvement. She went everywhere with us in her baby carrier. Serena Grace was about ten weeks old when she participated in the first of many Crim events to come before she could crawl.

Race morning was full of new experiences. Waiting in the throng of runners wasn't bad, as runners are generally friendly people. They always encourage new runners. It's as if they know a secret they want to share. Thousands of cheering spectators lined the Crim course. The huge number of people in the various races amazed me that morning. I couldn't believe we lived in Flint for six years and knew very little about the Crim. We certainly never knew there were that many runners in all of Michigan. The spectators cheered us on and Serena was a star. I carried her in the baby knapsack while Shari fed her on the go. I was proud that I could carry Serena on my chest for five miles of brisk walking. My back, however, was not impressed and was even less impressed the next day. We didn't know then that the Crim Festival of Races would become a much bigger part of all of our lives. That first Crim race is still one of the best days I've ever had.

The following spring, a parent at the Montessori School where my wife works brought in some flyers advertising the Crim Training Program. The sign-up form was due in a week. On a whim, Shari called a few friends and asked co-workers if they would join the program with her, but no one could fit it in. She was about to give up, but thought maybe I would do it with her. She was aware of my tendency not to follow through on her exercise directives. I said yes, despite being her last choice and we were off to the races. I thought she was a bit crazy when she told me we should run the Crim ten-mile road race.

I was anxious and pretty sure we wouldn't be able to do it. I didn't believe that either of us had it in us, which is probably why I was Shari's last choice. I knew she had never run before and in fact was not an athlete of any kind. She had told me before that she would never run unless something was chasing her. She had tried to get me interested in a variety of other aerobic and fitness activities, but I had not made it past a few weeks in any of them, and besides, I hadn't run since high school.

We tackled a trial run around the block of our subdivision and both of us had to stop and walk, completely out of breath after only a minute or so. I looked back at the house to see how far we had jogged. It was less than a tenth of a mile. Only nine miles and nine-tenths to go, I thought with a groan and I wondered what I had agreed to. I knew we were toast, but I had said I would do it with her. We kept going and did a bit more each time in the two weeks before the Crim Training Program started.

The program provided a plan, a schedule, and education about many aspects of running. We were given water bottles, Crim running shirts, free race entries, and a book on the Galloway method of training, which introduced us to the run/walk concept. We were assigned to a group of fifteen-minute-per-mile couch potatoes and started off slow with frequent walk breaks. The group of strangers we met in the program soon became friends with a common goal: to finish the Crim.

Everything about the program and the run/walk method were new to us. In the past when I tried to run for fitness, I always went out too often or set unrealistic start-up goals. My back or my knees would give me a clear message to go back inside and get out the chips and TV remote. Running alone was boring, and I always quit within a few weeks in a flurry of ibuprofen and Gatorade.

Many times early in the program people expressed doubts that they could finish, but the group enthusiasm and support always kept us going. We got the right shoes and new running clothes and learned how to avoid injuries. The walk breaks allowed us to build up our mileage slowly and socialize during workouts. Halfway through the program, the ten-mile race seemed like a possibility. We could actually finish it.

On race day thousands of runners and spectators filled downtown Flint. The sheer mass of colorfully dressed runners of all skill levels was awe inspiring. We were excited, well trained, and ready. In a few months we had gotten into the best shape we had been in for years.

I ran with my new friend Tim, and my wife ran with Dana, her new friend from the group. I'll never forget running past the four-mile marker where some guy held up a sign that said "The Kenyans are finished!" I didn't care. We were out there, we had a goal, and the crowds cheered everyone, not just the elite runners. The spectators at the Crim are race fans, but many are also the family members and friends of the runners. I knew my in-laws and daughters would be at the last turn before the finish.

The people along the course provided water, music, high-fives, and loads of verbal encouragement. Just when we thought we couldn't keep up the pace, someone would offer to spray us with water or yell something inspiring. Tim and I ran the race by running two minutes, alternating with two minutes walking, just as we had for months in our training group. We stayed on our pace goal. We supported each other along the way. At the last turn before the bricks of Saginaw Street, I saw my personal cheering section and got a hug from both my girls which gave me the push my tired body needed. When we ran up the home stretch, we had just enough energy left to turn it on and sprint to the finish. The announcer made note of the "two Clydesdales striding in" as Tim and I ran down the last hundred yards. We felt like gazelles, but large, lumbering horses were likely closer to the mark. We smiled as we crossed the finish line and made our way to the after-race refreshments. The water, fruit, and Popsicles were coveted like the last food on a desert island. We went back to cheer for all our running friends from the group.

Since then, we have kept up the tradition of watching for and cheering on all the other runners we know as they finish a race, and they do the same for us.

We were hooked on the Crim and had a blast at the post-race celebration. It's hard to walk well after running ten miles, but we actually danced! We took advantage of the grilled chicken from the food tent, and like all Crim champions, had a beer. Our kids played on the rides at the mini-carnival. The post-race music entertainment was first rate, and we spent the bulk of the day celebrating before going home to a shower and a well-deserved nap. The muscle ache was a good sort of pain, associated with accomplishment. I don't know about "runner's high," but I do know about "runner's nap."

From 2001 forward, my wife and I and the group have stayed with the Crim Training Program every year. We continue to improve as runners and support each other through tough times. We meet after some runs for a drink and a meal or to celebrate a birthday. Our whole group still runs the Crim every year as well as more than ten other local races. Several of us have finished half-marathons, and some have completed marathons.

We have gone from a group of out-of-shape couch potatoes to real runners, and loved every minute of it. Few sports allow you to run the same course on the same day as world-class athletes. Last year I almost got to the six-mile marker before the Kenyans were finished. I never see a Kenyan on the Crim course, but I see a great many friends.

The best part of running is the friendship and camaraderie with other runners. My best times and fondest memories come from running, now. Serena is now four years old. She and our eleven-year-old daughter Alaina have entered the Teddy Bear Trot and other local races for kids, and we have become a running family. My wife was thirty-four weeks pregnant for the 2004 Crim, so our newest addition, Mia, participated in the Crim before she was even born.

I've lost more than ten pounds, and our group as a whole has probably lost the weight equivalent of an entire person. I eat better foods because I actually care what I put in my body. I can't eat junk all the time, or the guy who juggles basketballs while he runs or the people with baby strollers would pass me. I have partially embraced nutrition, but I can still eat a half a bag of chips or a huge breakfast after a race. I still like to think root beer and cheese curls count as carbohydrate loading.

I look forward to all the races. I have recaptured the running spirit I had in high school. I love the peace of mind I feel when running. I am in the best shape I've been in for decades. I have my wife and the Crim Training Program to thank for my new running passion. It has brought us closer together as a family and as a group of friends with a common goal: run the Crim every year and enjoy one of the best days Flint has to offer.

CRIM FACT:
THE CRIM TEN-MILE COURSE RECORD FOR WOMEN WAS SET IN 1989 BY AMERICAN CATHY O'BRIEN. SHE FINISHED IN 51:47.

IT'S NOT HOW FAST YOU RUN, JUST RUN

BARBARA BESSO

AGE: 53
YEARS RUNNING: 1
CRIM FINISHES: 1
YEARS IN CTP: 1
RESIDENCE: GRAND BLANC, MI
OCCUPATION: REGISTERED NURSE

Eight years ago I was battling a serious autoimmune condition called scleroderma, which caused grinding pain in my hips with walking. I was very short of breath with minimal exertion. I couldn't even walk the dog. With prayers and nutritional supplements, my scleroderma is only a bad memory, but my habit of not exercising stuck with me.

In the spring of 2003, my twenty-three-year-old daughter entered the Crim ten-mile training program.

She encouraged me to think about it for the next year, because, as she put it, "There are a lot of women heavier and older than you in my group, and if they can do it, so can you."

I went out a few times with her and could not run for more than thirty seconds without being completely out of breath. I was fifty-one years old, overweight, and had never run farther than across the street since high school.

Physical fitness was never stressed for girls back in the 1960s. I could not run around a quarter mile track, even back then.

Last year I told my daughter "I'll join the Crim training team next year," just to get her to stop bugging me about it.

Well, next year came, and the sign-up form for the training program arrived in the mail. I signed up for the 8K. I thought I had better do it gradually. I could not persuade any of my friends to run it with me. My daughter was going to run the ten-mile again. I thought about backing out, because I wouldn't know anybody. Fortunately, I ended up in the slowest of the 8K groups, group AA. It was great to know there were others out there who had never run before.

I first realized I had a different mindset two weeks before the Crim. I thought our group would be running five miles. We had run four and a half the week before.

I came home and said to my husband, with a disappointed sound, "We *only* did four miles tonight." When I realized those words had come out of *my* mouth, I was shocked. *I had changed!*

My husband trained with me during the week, but he was unable to attend the Tuesday group sessions. He ran in the Crim with me and stayed with me the entire distance, even though he could have run a lot faster. I did it!

I know everyone says it's not important how fast you run, just that you do it. Well, my goal for next year is to improve my time, and I might even consider doing the ten-mile race.

Barb has been an R.N. for thirty two years. For the last ten years, she has worked for Genesys Home Health and Hospice. Barb is interested in, and sells nutritional supplements. She credits her Mannatech supplements for getting her to the finish line of her first Crim pain free. She has joined the training program again this year and plans to complete the ten-mile race in 2005.

WITH A LITTLE HELP FROM MY FRIENDS

MARGO MILLER

AGE: 48
YEARS RUNNING: 1
CRIM FINISHES: 1
YEARS IN CTP: 1
RESIDENCE: FLINT, MI
OCCUPATION: REGISTERED NURSE

This was my first year in the Crim Training Program. I guess I joined for many reasons. I signed up for the training program, thinking I was going to retire from work in July and it would give me something to do to keep busy the first couple of months of retirement. I thought it would be a bonus to lose weight, lower my cholesterol, decrease my body fat, and I hoped to meet some good people who would keep me motivated.

I had a rough time in the beginning of the training because after the first two weeks, I was hospitalized for five days. I called my group leader, Dave Whidden, from the hospital and told him I wasn't going to make it that week. He asked me if I was sure I couldn't make it! I again told him I was in the hospital, and even if I was discharged, I didn't think I could make it, because of how exhausted I was.

When I was discharged from the hospital, I had about six messages on my answering machine. Dave and my other trainer, Kim, called four times to check on me and tell me that the whole group would work with me to get me in shape. They each called again several times during the next two weeks that I missed training sessions. When I returned to my running group practice, everyone welcomed me and encouraged me. I was so impressed with their kind gestures that I e-mailed Dorie at the Crim office to let her know that the training group far surpassed any expectations I ever had. I also told her to pass the story on to whomever she wanted, to let the other trainers know that the little things they do go a long, long way.

The day before the Crim, one of my friends at work started a joke. She told everyone I was running the concession stand at the Crim this year and not to believe that I was actually running in the race. A lot of people asked me how I got my job at the Crim. I didn't know what they were talking about until someone told me who spread that rumor. When the race was done, I called the person at work and told her how I had done. She told me how proud she was of me, but quickly added, "Where are the treats from the concession stand?"

Now back to my reasons; well, I did not lose weight and my cholesterol actually went up, but I did meet some great people. I ran this year for the first time in my life. I ended up doing the 8K race in 1:03:13, just under a thirteen-minute mile. Not bad for a beginner! And yes, I did take the paper to work to prove that I actually did run in the race! Will I be back next year? Oh, yeah!

Margo is a registered nurse and works in the city that is the home of the Crim. In 2004, she participated in the Crim Training Program for the first time. She had never run before joining the program. She completed her goal race, the 8K run, and looks forward to training with the group again in 2005.

Unexpected Journey

ANDREW GRIFFIN

AGE: 47

YEARS RUNNING: 5

CRIM FINISHES: 4

YEARS IN CTP: 5

RESIDENCE: FLINT, MI

OCCUPATION: GRIFFIN FLOOR
COMPANY

"For a short guy Andy sure is getting paunchy" are not the words you want to hear about yourself. Or at least they weren't the words I wanted to hear about myself. As a matter of fact, that overheard sentence drove me crazy and replayed in my head over and over for weeks. Five years later the vision of one elderly great-uncle plopped on a folding chair in some relative's basement, celebrating somebody's birthday or anniversary or something, a paper plate of potato salad and empty chicken bones in his lap, casually gossiping about my apparently recent physical failings, to some equally elderly great-aunt, well, it can still bring me sitting up drenched in sweat from out of a deep sleep. For weeks I obsessed over that overheard scrap of conversation. I replayed it, and tried to dissect it from every angle. Isn't there an old saying that nobody overhears anything good said about himself?

I wasn't getting paunchy; I was just filling out. For crying out loud, when I graduated from high school I was so short and skinny I was still buying my pants in the little boys department. I was about to turn forty; of course I was gaining weight. Didn't my older relatives say our metabolism changes once you get past thirty? Didn't all my brothers' buddies have their annual changing-of-the-pants ceremony where the one with the largest waist bought new jeans and passed the outgrown pants down to the one with the next largest waist and so on down? And for that matter, who was Uncle Joe to be casting stones at anyone else's spare tire?

Worse yet, from a grammatical standpoint, "For a short guy Andy sure is getting paunchy" made absolutely no sense. It gave me great pleasure to picture my teachers and college instructors lined up at a blackboard demolishing that sentence.

Yet, I couldn't shake the gnawing feeling that there was an element of truth to Uncle Joe's words, that all the cold hard logic and debunking in the world would not nullify. It started a chain reaction. One random overheard unsettling sentence slowly but totally changed my life for the better. Six years later I am twenty pounds lighter, three waist sizes smaller, and more muscled and sinewy that I could have imagined. I routinely wear clothes I would have shrank from five years ago. I have a display case of medals for running distances that would have left me exhausted even imagining myself walking them. I've freakin' run marathons! I have run multiple marathons, enough that I can be pretentious and blasé about the subject. Best yet, I've spent hundreds of wonderful hours running miles with dozens of amazing new friends, people whose support and friendship will still be with me twenty years after I'm dead and buried.

I never planned this change. One step led me to the next step by random accident. Not until a few years had passed, did I realize that I had completely renovated my life and that I was doing things I would have bet my soul against a few years earlier.

Everything comes back to "For a short guy Andy sure is getting paunchy." Once I realized I wasn't going to be able to dismiss those words I wondered what I would have to do to lose that paunch. I fished an old pair of tennis shoes out of the back closet, and one quiet Sunday afternoon I jogged for a few blocks around the neighborhood. It wasn't that bad. Small children didn't taunt me with, "Hey, old fat guy!" like I'd imagined they would. I didn't pass out in a neighbor's driveway. People smiled and waved at me as I slowly ran by. The neighborhood looked nicer and more interesting from outside my car than it did when I drove through it.

I was proud of myself in spite of my lack of ambition. I rarely ran for more than thirty minutes. I never left my subdivision and rarely ran two days in a row. Still, within a few weeks I'd already lost five pounds and my jeans fit again. If I ran farther and more often, could I lose ten or more pounds and get back to my old waist size? By then I was running around the block for twenty-five minutes three times a week. I'd find the old me again.

Instead I found a new me. At yet another of those minor family functions I opened my mouth to brag and found myself taunted into the next step. My kid sister told me I could run around the block all I wanted, but she was entering me in a charity 5K race in her hometown. Not only did she expect me to show up and run all three-plus miles, but she also expected me to do it in less than half an hour. Or else! Little sisters are a scary breed. How could she do that to me?

I was a nerve case. Who knew what would happen? I imagined all sorts of scary scenarios.

Instead, running in a crowd of a thousand people was a blast! Yes it was scary, it hurt, and I'd never run that far. I probably came in 999th. On the other hand, there was something uplifting about being in a crowd of people moving forward with one common goal, with a thousand different bodies of differing abilities, each runner with his or her own story. Oh yeah, I managed to break a half hour with a few seconds to spare. Take that little sister! She still finished several minutes ahead of me, but I planned to practice a little harder and close the gap the next year.

That was an October race, and by July, I was feeling cocky. My bank had a stack of Crim Festival of Race entry forms lying on the counter. Surely all the real runners were doing the ten-mile road race. So I could enter the 5K and who would notice? I mailed in my filled application before I had the chance to think twice. I ran the Crim 5K in August. I ran the Toledo 5K in October. I was barely faster, but I loved the crowds, and I loved the challenge.

In my Crim entry packet was a flyer for yet another 5K race. Didn't running through Kensington Metro Park on a brisk autumn morning sound nice in a wholesome way? At that race was a picnic table full of flyers for other races. There were more? Some races were right around the corner from me. And at every race I found flyers for more races. Wow, had this stuff been going on all this time?

That New Year's I made a resolution. I would pre-register for one race each month. I would pin the entries on my refrigerator and always have a reminder in front of me, daring me to close that door without grabbing a high-calorie snack. It kept me honest. Knowing I had paid to run a race in two weeks kept me running regularly. I was beginning to recognize the other faces at the back of the crowd, and I wanted to improve.

One day I opened my mailbox and amid the catalogues was a flyer for the Crim Training Program. I tossed it into a pile with my other junk mail. Eventually I skimmed the flyer and threw it into my wastebasket. Pay $120 to spend 16 weeks running with other people? That sounded a lot like gym class. Hadn't I been the boy who ducked out of high school gym class by faking a doctor's note informing the world that I had the first known case of male menstrual cramps? What were these Crim people thinking?

The next Saturday I came home from my monthly 5K race. Once again I had struggled to break twenty-nine minutes for a 3.1-mile race. I wasn't getting any faster. I fished the Crim Training Program application out of my trash basket to reread it. It seemed sensible, and they were throwing in a ton of wonderful extras. Yes, I was the proverbial lone wolf, but would it kill me to run with other people one night a week for a couple of weeks? I wasn't getting any better running on my own. How could they make me any worse? The next question was: Which subprogram would I enter? I wasn't an experienced ten-mile runner. I'd never run more than four miles. I'd done nearly a dozen 5Ks by then, so the beginner 5K program seemed wrong. That left only the beginner ten-mile program. One major snag: I had no intention of running a ten-mile race. They couldn't make me run ten-miles. I wouldn't do that. That was crazy.

Orientation night had me nervous. What was I getting myself into? I left the gym feeling rather reassured. The speakers were wonderful and their enthusiasm pumped me up.

I was even more nervous on the sorting night. I was expected to run in public with a group of strangers. We are back to the humiliation of high school gym. Well, we were only going to run a mile. I'd run three-mile races, so a mile was nothing, right? I ran, it was fun, and I was surprised to learn I was assigned to the fastest beginner ten-mile group. I did the math. Eighty-five percent of the beginner ten-milers were slower than me!

My new group met and I panicked again. My group leaders didn't seem as smiley and friendly as the other group leaders. The other runners in my group looked younger and fitter than I did. I was convinced I was going to hate these people. Worse yet, I figured once we got past three miles, I was going to drop dead and everyone would run past my lifeless corpse, making fun of how flabby I looked.

Sometimes it is nice to be wrong. My leaders were wonderful. My group members didn't seem to notice that I was older and less fit than the rest of them. I found myself arriving early on Tuesday nights so I could chat with the other runners. I did not drop dead.

My group leaders explained we were training with walking intervals. We would run three minutes then walk one minute, over and over, until we finished. Knowing I had to run only three minutes reassured me. I had to hang in for only three minutes, and then I could rest. Running became less daunting. The longest distance became no more than just pieces of running and walking.

My group ran beyond four miles, and nothing terrible happened to me. I was running longer distances than I had ever imagined in my life. Five miles! Six miles! Eight miles! Maybe I could run a ten-mile race. I wouldn't be fast, but I could do it.

Within two months of Crim training, I ran my monthly 5K races much faster! By June I not only was finishing under twenty-eight minutes, but I was also crossing the finish line under twenty-seven minutes. Other runners I knew only by sight came up to me after races to congratulate me on my improvement!

I'm never calm very long. By July I was back to freaking out. Could I really run a ten-mile race? One Saturday morning I rolled out of bed, put on shorts and shoes, and left my house. Two hours later I jogged into my parents' driveway, eleven and a half miles down the road. If I could do that on my own, then I could handle ten miles surrounded by other runners. The training had worked.

I survived the long runs with my group. I survived the nights we ran in sticky hot weather. I survived runs where my body was exhausted from working all day. Running with my new friends seemed to revitalize me every Tuesday. I was meeting people. At the races I knew other beginner runners, and I was less alone in the crowds at the starting line. When I finished, friends waited to cheer me, and there were friends for me to cheer on.

I ran the Crim ten-mile road race! I will never forget the huge crowds running with me every step of the race. There were more people than in any other race I had ever run! Just as wonderful were all the spectators on the sidewalk and volunteers passing out water. Yes, running ten miles was hard, but I was doing it! Around the halfway mark I realized not only was I going to easily break two hours, I could also break ninety minutes if I stayed steady. "Must not weaken," I thought. Me, the pudgy un-athletic guy was running a ten-mile race! I did break ninety minutes, by only by a few seconds, but I felt like an Olympic athlete. I wore my finishers medal the rest of the day. I carried it with me and showed it to everyone for weeks. I pulled it out of my pocket to shamelessly impress clerks at the grocery store, video store, and dry cleaner. I hung my medal from my rear view mirror as if it was St. Christopher.

Although I'd worried at the beginning because I was the oldest, least fit member of my group, I ran the second fastest time of my entire group. I had found my *inner jock*.

I'm not a social man, but I attended the Crim Training Program's Victory Party the following Tuesday. I had to spend one last night with my group. I listened to all the stories as they passed a microphone. We had all accomplished much more than we expected. It felt like a religious experience. I felt honored to have been part of the Crim Training Program. I was glad I hadn't thrown out that application.

At the Victory Party I learned some runners were meeting informally on Tuesday nights downtown come fall. I had come too far to stop now. I was there the next Tuesday, and most Tuesdays afterwards, still meeting new friends.

A group of veteran runners told me they ran downtown on Thursday nights and I was welcome to join them. I felt like I'd been asked to the junior prom or something. By then I was running two nights a week with other people, plus meeting friends at races. I was going out afterwards with friends, we were making phone calls to check in with each other during the week, and I was constantly meeting new people. Me, Mr. Anti-social, liked nearly every one I ran with. I was attending weddings, christenings, funerals, and concerts with these people. As a bonus I'd lost twenty pounds and was fitter than ever before in my life.

My third year of running I ran my first half-marathon in the spring, 13.1 miles! That fall friends suggested we all run a marathon together, 26.2 miles. I wasn't that crazy! Still, these were running friends and their company meant a lot to me.

Next thing I knew I had entered the Chicago Marathon. I prepared using all the ideas I'd learned training for the Crim. I told no one I knew before I left that I'd entered this. What if I failed? Instead, it was the coolest experience of my life. I finished in the middle of the pack! I ran a 26.2 mile race!

Now I run four times a week with groups of fascinating folks. I run alone only when I feel a rare need for a solitary test. My times vary, but six years later, I continue getting faster over longer distances.

Nothing has changed, but everything has changed. Every season I meet new people running, yet I'm still doing things with friends I met in all my Crim training groups. The last two years I've led Crim training groups, hoping to share the joy I experienced.

Three years since the Uncle Joe comment and I've run seven marathons. The Olympics will never call, and I'm probably too slow to qualify for the Boston Marathon, but I'm going to keep running. I love it.

The friendly competition between Andrew and I has made us both better runners. Andrew is not only an excellent runner, he is a good cook. He is always invited to parties because he makes us laugh and brings good food. One year we were celebrating his birthday and we didn't know his age. One of us looked it up on the internet results of a local race. Unknown to us, they made a mistake and listed his age as fifty. We got him "Happy 50th" cards and marveled at how good he looked for fifty. It turns out he was only forty-four. To add insult to injury, we forgot to tell him about the party. All of us showed up at a local restaurant to celebrate his fiftieth, and no one had told Andrew. Needless to say, he was less amused than the rest of us, but suffered through it with his usual wit.

CHAPTER THREE
The Streakers

TWENTY YEARS
AND COUNTING

BILL HARRIS

AGE: 55
YEARS RUNNING: 22
CRIM FINISHES: 22
RESIDENCE: GRAND BLANC, MI
OCCUPATION: NEWS ANCHOR, ABC 12

The year was 1981, and I had just purchased a house in a peaceful neighborhood on the west side of Flint. It was a humid, quiet Saturday August morning when I awoke to the odd sound of laughter and clapping. I peered out my bedroom window and became wide-eyed at the site of hundreds of scantily clad men and women passing by my front door. I thought, "Who are these people, and what are they doing?"

Wanting to investigate further, I grabbed my lawn chair, a box of doughnuts, a cold beverage, and headed for my front lawn. That was my first introduction to the Crim. Three years later I gave up my lawn chair, donned a pair of running shoes, and along with my wife and brother-in-law, ran my first ten-mile event. Two hundred miles and twenty consecutive races later, I've recorded a lifetime of wonderful memories.

Two years, in particular, stand out. My inaugural race year was 1984. Somewhere around the four-mile mark, I developed a pain in my right ankle. My wife, who's my Crim coach and running partner, took notice and quietly devised a plan to take my mind off the pain. When we approached the bottom of the Bradley hills, just a block from our front door, Jane chose that moment to tell me she was pregnant with child number two! As we passed our house, just beyond the five-mile marker, both of us shouted the news to my wife's parents and our seven-month-old daughter, all of who were watching the race on our front lawn. I was still in shock at the time. The experience brought new meaning to the phrase, "No Pain. No Gain."

Another significant year in my life was 1989, the dreaded year some family members and friends *insisted* on recalling the fortieth anniversary of my birth. Worse yet, the actual date of number forty took place on Crim day. My wife went to great lengths to make sure the milestone did not go unnoticed. The morning began at the starting line with my wife/running partner dressed in black, complete with black veil, and wearing a sign that read, "Lordy, Lordy, Look Who's 40" with an arrow pointing in my direction. We approached the first mile marker, and saw in the distance a sign similar to the Burma Shave roadside signs of the 1940s and 1950s. As I got closer, I made out the letters "B-I-L-L" followed by "L-O-R-D-Y, L-O-R-D-Y..."

For the next nine miles, every mile marker was adorned with a similar birthday greeting. Of course, no birthday party would be complete without cake and balloons. My wife and I slowed our pace long enough to share a piece of cake with family members who were camped out at the five-mile mark. When we returned to the pack, I was handed several black balloons that were still floating above my head as I passed through the Saginaw Street chutes.

Along with 5,000 of my closest friends, I will forever recall my sixth Crim ten-mile. That year I celebrated my fortieth birthday, and, on the very same day, ran in a *Master's* Division for the first time.

Bill Co-anchors the 6 and 11 P.M. news on WJRT-TV ABC 12 (Flint-Saginaw-Bay City) along with fellow Crim

Runner Angie Schramski. Bill is a Massachusetts native and joined the WJRT-TV staff in 1977. He and his wife, Jane, live in Grand Blanc. Bill also identifies Jane as his running partner and coach. They have two children, Nicole and Christopher, and a pet dog, "Teddy".

CRIM FACT:
IN 2004, THE MALE MASTER'S WINNER
PLACED 5TH OVERALL.

HOOK, LINE, AND SINKER

MALISSA LAUDERBAUGH

AGE: 36
YEARS RUNNING: 24
CRIM FINISHES: 20
RESIDENCE: FLINT, MI
OCCUPATION: EMPLOYED BY A
   HEATING AND A/C WHOLESALER

I was a track runner in the seventh grade at Kearsley Middle School. I was a hurdler, believe it or not. My eighth grade year, I was the number-one hurdler in the Big Nine. It was an accomplishment I was proud of, but my freshman year at the high school, I went from being number one to just about dead last in the hurdlers. The older, stronger, more experienced runners beat me every time. I was discouraged. I barely managed to squeak by and get my varsity letter that year.

To my continued disappointment, my sophomore year was not any better. The only good thing I had going for me was that I turned out to be a strong high jumper. Another factor that influenced my hurdling was that I had put on weight. It was weight I didn't need, but that I had acquired through poor eating habits.

After my sophomore year, I decided the summer before my junior year that I was going to give up hurdling and go out for Cross Country. Every day in the summer I went out and ran the 3.5-mile route I had created for myself. I couldn't run the entire thing at first. I had to take walk breaks. It was tough on really hot days, but I forced myself to do it. Eventually I could run the entire distance without stopping.

In August, I joined the Cross Country team and completed all the workouts. I wasn't the strongest runner, but I wasn't the worst one, either. I continued to improve and lost the extra weight I had put on.

When I decided to run my first Crim, I was sixteen years old. I hadn't run farther than five or six miles in my Cross Country practices. I am not sure what made me want to run that first Crim, I just decided I was going to and figured I could finish. That was my goal. In my first Crim, which started on Robert T. Longway near the Mott Skill Trade Building, I was awestruck at the huge size of the race. I had never seen so many runners in a race. There must have been more than 500 runners in my first Crim. I did finish. If I remember correctly, my time was in the ninety-minute range. I felt very satisfied with my effort.

The summer prior to my senior year, I began thinking about the Crim again. I decided what the heck, I did it once. I was a much faster and stronger runner than I was the year before. I took it as a challenge to see how much time I could shave off from the year before. I added some longer runs that summer. I was confident I could do better, and I did. I finished the Crim that year in eighty-six minutes, which spurred me on.

After graduation from high school, I decided to set a goal for myself to run ten consecutive Crims. How or why I ever came up with that goal, I do not know. I was a goal-oriented person, I suppose. An added plus was that it would keep me running for eight more Crim races. The crowd of runners, the wonderful volunteers, and the terrific support from people along the course made the Crim an exciting thing to do each year. Each summer, I looked forward to the Crim, whether I was at my best or not. I had some grand events, and, unfortunately, obstacles to overcome as well.

One year I got married in September and adopted my stepson. My father had to have part of his aorta replaced the following summer. Two years later, in August, my father had a five-vessel bypass on his heart and almost did not make it. I had three ectopic pregnancies in six months. The first one almost killed me, because of internal bleeding. The second one was in July. The third one was right after the Crim.

A few years later, in September, we adopted three children after five unsuccessful years of trying to start a family. I ran my first marathon in Detroit with my father-in-law, who decided to start running after watching me finish one of my Crims. Despite all this, I still managed to complete my goal. I managed to finish ten consecutive Crims.

After I finished my tenth Crim, I must have been delirious, because I revised my goal. I decided that because I finished ten consecutive Crims, I'd do it again and go for twenty. At some point in my first ten Crims, the race start line was moved to downtown Flint in front of the hotel that has changed names many times over the years. Over time, other race distances were added. It seemed that each year for several years, a new race distance was added, and the Crim just kept growing and growing. Each year the Crim ten-mile race kept gaining more and more runners. It was exciting to go each year and see so many new runners as the race grew in size and popularity.

Along the way over the years, a runner could be seeded. This meant if you ran the Crim or a 10K at a certain race pace, you could start at the very front of the pack, just behind the world-class runners. With effort, determination, and a little luck, I managed to get seeded. It is an honor to be seeded, the best part of which is admiring the world-class runners and talented local runners and friends up front.

The second ten years of running the Crim ten-miler had its ups and downs, just like the first ten years did. I finally graduated from college, as I worked full time and went to school at night. I qualified for the Boston Marathon, and by doing so, reached another of my running goals. My father-in-law, who was my best friend, suddenly passed away. I changed careers. I went through a divorce. Through everything the Crim and my running were always there for me.

For several Crims, I managed to keep breaking my personal best times like many other beginning runners. There were a few years that my Crim times were not as strong. As in other years, running and racing had its ups and downs just like life.

My divorce had taken a toll on me. The stress was too much for my body. I came down with a blood virus that caused me trouble for almost three years. During that time, my thyroid went on the fritz and became overactive. I have to take medication to keep it in check. I had asthma so bad one summer that my lung capacity went below fifty percent. At one point, the lung specialist thought I had lung cancer, based on results of X-rays and CAT scans. Thank goodness, I didn't. No matter what obstacle came my way, I never veered from my goal. Each year I kept training. Each year I finished the Crim ten-miler.

This year was my twentieth consecutive Crim ten-mile road race. I almost thought I wasn't going to run this Crim. I unexpectedly had to have my appendix removed in July. Just about the time that I recovered from the appendectomy, I had to have my gall bladder taken out six weeks later. Those surgeries didn't stop me from achieving my goal in the Crim, two useless organs lighter.

You already know what happened after I achieved my original goal in the Crim, after finishing my twentieth Crim, I made a new goal. I have always admired the few runners who have run in and finished all twenty-eight Crims. My new goal is to keep running the Crim every year until I can't run the Crim anymore. I fully expect to double the goal I already accomplished and then some. What can I say? I am hooked!

The truth is it really isn't the goal that keeps me running in the Crim each year. In part, I love running. But the main reason I run the Crim each year is because, well, it is THE CRIM. The Crim is Flint. It is a time for all of Flint, the surrounding areas, women, and men, children of any race, religion, or social status, to come together as one. The Crim is a bond that brings all of us together, not just the runners but also all the wonderful volunteers and all those fantastic supporters along the course. I am in awe each year when I look at all the people who come together to work as a team to make the event one of the most successful races in the country. It is an event that everyone looks forward to, whether runners or not. All you have to do, any time of the year, is say "The Crim" to someone in Flint, and it puts a smile on his or her face. The Crim is something all of us can be proud of, because it is something we have accomplished together. It has taken all of us to make the Crim the successful race it is today. Apparently I am not the only one who is hooked!

Malissa is a working, single-parent of two children, Brandon and Ashley. She has taken pride in running and finishing the Crim twenty consecutive times. Malissa believes running is a gift that should never be taken for granted. The Crim has become a family event and each year Malissa runs the ten-mile, Brandon runs the 8K and Ashley runs the 5K race. It won't be long before there are two more ten-mile runners in the Crim.

MEMORIES OF THE CRIM

KAREN BELL

AGE: 63
YEARS RUNNING: 28
CRIM FINISHES: 27
RESIDENCE: OTISVILLE, MI
OCCUPATION: RETIRED SPECIAL EDUCATION
  TEACHER

In 1978, at age thirty-six, I ran my first ten-mile Crim race. I have continued to run the ten-mile race every year since. Because the ten-mile was the only event when I started running the Crim, to run any other distance would not be the "true" Crim for me. I have many great memories as well as some memorabilia: most of the T-shirts, a few awards for placing in my age group, and the tongue depressor from the 1979 race. All finishers were given a depressor with their overall place on it.

One memorable race was the year it rained. Well, actually, it didn't just rain. There was a drenching downpour for the whole ten miles. When I finished I felt like I was carrying enough water in my shoes to fill a swimming pool.

In 2001, my daughter Kristine ran with me. She had given birth to our first grandchild just four weeks earlier. My other daughter, Laura, won some of the Michigan runner prize money a couple of times, and those years were very memorable for our family.

One year I spotted a former student of mine walking

at the eight-and-a-half-mile mark. He was about forty years my junior. When he saw that the "old lady" was going to beat him to the finish line, he found he had enough left to start running again and get to the finish line before I did. We had a good laugh about that.

Hitting the bricks on Saginaw Street is a great memory every year. It is wonderful to see the crowd welcoming the runners to the finish line. As a retired Special Education teacher, I saw the benefits of Special Olympics for some of my students. I can certainly appreciate the financial support the Crim race has given to this very worthy cause. Long live the Crim!

Karen has run in all of the ten-mile Crim races since 1978. She has placed in the top three of her age group four times. Karen has been married to husband, Curt, for forty years. They have two adult daughters, Kristine and Laura, who are both runners. They have four grandchildren.

CRIM FACT:
A "KENYON" WON THE INAUGURAL CRIM IN 1977.
IT WAS STEVE KENYON OF GREAT BRITAIN.

EVERY CRIM BUT ONE

JOHN JEROME

AGE: 49
YEARS RUNNING: ABOUT 32
CRIM FINISHES: 27
RESIDENCE: LINDEN, MI
OCCUPATION: PROJECT MANAGER

The summer of 1977 I trained three or four days for the inaugural Crim. When the race started, high noon on race day, I was standing on the crosswalk from the Mott Community College parking ramp to the campus. Below me passed everyone who had done what I had not; signed up for the first-ever Bobby Crim ten-mile road race. One of the people to pass below me was my high school cross-country coach from Kearsley, Larry Witze. Little did I know, watching that race would change my life.

In 1978, one day before the second Crim, a good friend of mine named Dan Heady asked if I wanted to run the Crim with him the next day. Dan and I had played many games of racquetball that year, but I had not run much.

I said, "Sure."

We ran the Crim, and both of us finished in the upright position. At that point I was hooked. The next year, Hurley Hospital started a race called the Tuuri 10,000, named after a prominent local pediatrician. I ran the Crim and the Tuuri 10K in 1979. I was getting my running legs.

Over the years I have met many wonderful people through running. I am lucky to be able to call Lois Craig my friend. Lois, along with Bobby Crim, started the great Crim race. A few years back I was running the Crim and was at about the seven-mile mark and looked over to the side and saw Bobby Crim running along. People were passing him unaware that they were out there running that great race thanks to Bobby and Lois. Being the shy person that I am, I made an announcement in a loud, clear voice for all to hear: "*Hey! This man is Bobby Crim,*" I yelled. Several people around us took note, and Bobby smiled.

At the 10-year anniversary of the Crim, the *Flint Journal* took a picture of everyone who had run all ten Crims. If only I had trained and paid my entry fee, I would have been included in that original group. As it was, I had officially run only nine in a row.

Back around 1995, I received a flyer about the Crim Training Program. I called up John and Anne Gault to talk with them about the program and find out how to sign up. Anne informed me that I did not want to be in the training program; I wanted to be a trainer. I thank Anne to this day for setting me straight. Over the next six years I, along with many others, had the pleasure of helping people train to run ten miles.

I met former Olympian Jeff Galloway several times. During one visit we talked about what it was like to be at the 1972 Munich Summer Olympics and participate in the opening ceremony. Another time we talked about Steve "Pre" Prefontaine. Jeff and "Pre" were at the Olympics together. A character plays Jeff in the movie about Steve's life.

In 1996, the Crim celebrated twenty years. Again they took a picture of everyone who had run twenty consecutive Crims. I noticed a good friend of mine, Jack Price, was in the picture. It was not mentioned in the article, but Jack had run all twenty Crims and had run all seventeen Tuuri 10K races, also. He was the only one to have accomplished this goal. I also noticed that the number of runners in the picture was smaller. The *Twenty-Crim Crew* was a more select group.

Since that day in 1978 when Dan enticed me to run my first Crim, the second running of the Crim, I have met many of the race directors. John and Anne Gault and Mark Bauman, of the Riverbend Striders, even helped me organize several local races. One was in Linden during the Summer Happening celebration, and the other was near the Hurley Health and Fitness Center. It was called the Towel Run.

You can run races, help at the check-in table, and even help at aid stations, but until you are in charge of putting on a race, you cannot realize all the work it takes to put together a race. To Lois Craig, Laurie McCann, Anne Gault, and Sherlynn Everly of the Crim and Dave Standridge, Carol McLearn, Kay Kelly, and Karen Kowalko of the Tuuri, I say "Thank you." To Bev Martin of the Crim, I would also say a special "Thank you" for all your help and kindness over the years.

Everyone who has ever run in a race should work at an aid station. Aid station workers are the unsung heroes of road races. One year while working for EDS, we sponsored an aid station near the corner of Bradley and Corunna. One of my co-workers had a child in the Swartz Creek Band and asked the band to come out and play at the aid station. We won best aid station that year. The aid station has gone away, but the band plays on. The boys and girls of the Swartz Creek High School Band now play on Parkside near the seven-mile mark.

At the twenty-fifth anniversary of the Crim it was easy to see that the group of runners that had run all the Crim races was getting smaller and smaller as the years went by. At the twenty-eighth anniversary of the Crim, I celebrated my twenty-fifth anniversary at the Tuuri. One day, and God willing it will be a long time from now, that hearty group that has finished all the Crims will have their string come to an end. Then those who missed the first year, like me, but competed every year since, will be able to claim they have the longest streak of consecutive Crims.

As you read this, do not misunderstand me. I do not wish any harm to anyone from that original group. I hope that when they are 100 years old, they can still run the Crim. They are the ones who have inspired me to keep going. Try to imagine the luck, the skill, and the ability that has enabled them to walk up to the starting line and run ten miles for more than twenty-five years in a row. Injuries and illness have come and gone, rainstorms and hellish heat have not stopped them. The Crim staff even moved the starting line, but these men on the fourth Saturday in August, have toed the line. It is an amazing feat, and I admire them all.

John was born and raised in the Flint area. He started ed running at Kearsley High School in the 1970s and has not stopped since. He is married, and has two children, a son and daughter. He organized running teams at McLaren Regional Medical Center, EDS, and General Motors. He tried his hand as race director of two local races with the local running club, The Riverbend Striders. He was one of the original twelve group leaders for the first Crim Training Program in 1995. To date, he has run every Tuuri 10K, all but the first Crim, and has completed six marathons.

CHAPTER FOUR
Funny Shorts

WATCH YOUR MOUTH
AND YOUR FEET

DENICE WAGNER

AGE: 47
YEARS RUNNING: 28
CRIM FINISHES: 14
YEARS IN CTP: 2
RESIDENCE: DAVISON, MI
OCCUPATION: EMPLOYED BY GM
  FOR 28 YEARS

DENICE

I just completed my fourteenth Crim. As I was running the course today, I found myself reminiscing about the first time I ran the Crim. I wasn't familiar with the course and had not driven the course in my vehicle before the race. I should have, because of all the horror stories I had heard about the Bradley hills.

At around the three-mile marker, I realized I had started out too fast and wouldn't finish unless I slowed down and paced myself.

Out of nowhere, a runner started talking to me about the pace we were running and offered to team up with me and complete the race together. As we made our way up the first Bradley hill, I said a few swear words. We made it through the Bradleys with great effort and continued our conversation when we could.

Between miles six and eight, I said a few more,

choice words about how no one had told me how difficult the hills were along the golf course. When we neared the end of the race, I asked my new supportive partner where he worked, and he replied, "I'm a Catholic Priest." Oops, all I could think about was the language I had used earlier when I was describing the grueling course!

Denice was born and raised in Davison and lives there with her husband of eighteen years, Terry. She has been running for twenty-eight years, and enjoys weekend runs with her local running group. She has completed fourteen Crim ten-mile road races and finished her first marathon in Traverse City in 2004. Her next goal is to run the Royal Victoria Marathon in Victoria, British Columbia.

To Laugh or to Cry

WALLY MCLAUGHLIN

AGE: 72
YEARS RUNNING: 30
CRIM FINISHES: 27
YEARS IN CTP: 10
RESIDENCE: FLUSHING, MI
OCCUPATION: RETIRED RETAIL
  STORE OWNER

Several years ago, a program called "Coming Your Way" let folks who lived along the Crim route know what to expect. Lots of volunteers walked along the path of the Crim with flyers and friendly attitudes spreading the news.

At the Sunset Apartment complex on the Bradley hills we walked down the hallways knocking on doors, giving out flyers, talking to people, and moving on. At one particular door, I knocked and received no response, so I slid a flyer under the door.

Suddenly, a voice, an elderly voice from a woman perhaps in her 80s, said "Yeeessss, whaaaat issss it?"

I thought to myself, "Oh, boy, how am I going to explain this?"

With my best enunciation, I said, "I wanted to let you know I put a flyer under your door telling you there's a race coming by here on Saturday."

The little old lady inside answered, "Are you crazy or something? I can hardly get around my apartment and you want me to run in a race?"

Wally lives in Flushing with his wife and two Golden Labrador Retrievers. He owned a Ben Franklin dime store prior to retiring and has always been physically active. Now he has more time for biking, kayaking and skiing, but he feels running is "tops". He describes the positive relationships from running as gifts and he is grateful for the resulting friendships and his continued ability to run. Due to a death in the family, Wally missed one Crim race or he would have completed them all.

He has a complete collection of Crim T-shirts. He was gracious enough to let me to visit with him and photograph the T-shirt logos for the color photo section of this book.

One year he recalls driving the Kenyan elite runners through the Bradley hills for a pre-race tour of the course. He implied that the Kenyans shrugged and said, "Is that it?" Perhaps Kenyan hills are steeper.

TIGHTLY MATCHED

ANTHONY ELLIS

Courtesy of brightroom

AGE: 41
YEARS RUNNING: 5
CRIM FINISHES: 4
YEARS IN CTP: 4
RESIDENCE: FLUSHING, MI
OCCUPATION: GERIATRIC PSYCHIATRIST

One of the consequences of becoming a runner and running the Crim every year has been developing a fascination with running clothes. Early on when I was searching for running clothes, I was looking for function over form or style. I liked the pants with zippered pockets and places to put money, keys, and such. For a while I was interested in the idea of a shirt that had a pocket on it that I could put my running number in, so I wouldn't have to use those darned little pins.

Unfortunately, my interest in running clothes became a strange obsession. When I shop for running clothes now, I look at the colors and the patterns and have developed an idea that they have to match. You won't see me wearing an old pair of gym shorts or a leftover bathing suit. No, I'm a running fashion mogul. One year, I was preparing for the Tuuri and striving to draw on the running clothes to shave a bit of time off my prior year's effort. I put together an outfit that will live in infamy.

The shorts were red and black and had an exciting dynamic stripe along the side that merged into a similar stripe on the shirt in such a way as to create an ensemble that was beyond compare. I didn't stop there, though. I became fascinated with the idea that *everything had to match*, and thus purchased a new pair of running shoes. The new shoes were also marked with red and black and gave the impression of forward motion at a speed not likely attainable by me. I wasn't finished yet. I bought a pair of red, white, and black socks that had a roadrunner on the side of the sock. The roadrunner had feathers on its head that were drawn back into a flame, again impressing upon the viewer the fierce speed with which I was likely to move. You would think that that would have been enough. It wasn't. I purchased special red shoelaces that allowed me to lace the shoes in such a way that I didn't have to tie the shoes anymore, but instead simply slipped them on. I thought they would save time on race morning and wouldn't come untied during my pre-Crim Tuuri 10K effort.

The socks should have been the coup de grace for my red-and-black greased-lightning ensemble, but as you can probably tell from this story so far, I was out of control. For some reason, I believed that I needed a headband. Not just any headband. It had to match. I went to two stores and finally found a gray tie-on headband that had a red stitched logo sewn in. I did not try the headband on in the store, so I had no idea what it would look like when I put it on. I knew it was a necessary component for my "speedwear."

I was ready. I had matching pants, shirt, shoes, socks, and headband. I was certain the overall effect would be a stunning testament to my running fashion sense. The new clothes would clearly allow me to shave thirty to sixty seconds off my previous Tuuri time, just from the sheer psychological boost of wearing such a stunning $200 outfit. At the very least, my wallet was lighter.

On the morning of Tuuri race day, which is a common 10K preparation race for the Crim, I came out of the bathroom in my speed ensemble and ran straight into my wife, who looked at me aghast.

She said, "Oh my god, Buster, you're not going to wear that, are you?"

"What do you mean? Of course I am."

She said, "All you need to top that off is a pair of leg warmers. You look like the guy from River Dance."

I thought she was being a harsh critic and not a helpful spouse who was trying to save me from embarrassment.

Later our friend Keeley came over to take care of our youngsters while we went to the race. I found out that my wife's fashion assessment was not far off. Keeley didn't say anything when she saw me in my speed outfit; she simply laughed out loud and couldn't stop. After she wiped the tears from her eyes, I asked her what was so funny. She implied my outfit might get me noticed in a way that I had not intended.

I was flabbergasted and amazed at her attack on my running fashion sense and didn't know what to do. I went back in the bathroom and looked at the ensemble with a more critical eye. I reluctantly removed the headband, but was unwilling to make any further changes.

When I got to the start line, I found myself nervously looking around at other people's clothing. I noticed that very few *males* had tightly matched running outfits. I was a bit self-conscious and wondered if my wife and friend were right. I knew I was in trouble when someone whistled at me and there were no women close by.

Believe it or not, my story has a happy ending. I went to the Tuuri 10K that day, and beat my previous time by almost a minute. I was certain it was directly related to the roadrunner socks; however, when I was discussing my theory with Brian Barkey after the race, he informed me that it could have had something to do with the previous year's horrid and humid weather conditions and this year's perfect weather. I was not amused by his analysis because I had spent about $10 on those socks. Forever after, that particular outfit has lived in the shameful world of stupid ideas that seemed good at the time. Now everyone in my running group checks to make sure that they're not too color coordinated, especially the males. Sometimes I wonder what would have happened to my race time if I'd worn the headband.

CRIM FACT:
AVERAGE CRIM DAY TEMPERATURE IS SIXTY-SEVEN. THE COOLEST START WAS FIFTY-TWO DEGREES IN 1997, AND THE HOTTEST WAS NINETY DEGREES IN 1977.

ALMOST GOT NOTHING

KEELEY BYERLY

AGE: 43
YEARS RUNNING: 2
CRIM FINISHES: 1
YEARS IN CTP: 2
RESIDENCE: FLUSHING, MI
OCCUPATION: STUDENT NURSE

I started the Crim Training Program in May 2003. My catalyst for joining was the same as for many others. It was a major life event for me, divorce. I knew I needed a boost of confidence and had seen first-hand what a positive experience my friends Shari and Tony were having in the program.

Shari had always been fit but was the first to say, "You won't catch me running unless something's chasing me, and it better be big and it better be fast." I think she was more surprised than me when she finished her first Crim.

I was placed in group E with a bunch of strangers, which felt a little weird, but we got to know each other quickly. Each week we moaned and groaned, but we got our mileage in. Some weeks were a bit overwhelming. That's when these strangers, who by then were becoming dear friends, gave me the push I needed to continue.

The night we ran nine miles, it felt so easy, it was hard to believe. We all looked at each other and had a "Are you sure that was nine miles?" expression on our faces.

The Crim practice run was quite a different story. The first five miles flew by, as usual. When I hit the seven-mile marker, I was done like toast. My legs felt like lead. I had nothing left and had to walk the last three miles.

That summer I began to find my true self again. With each week and each mile, a little piece of the old me came back, and I was glad to see me again.

On the day of the Crim, the excitement of race day and the crowds carried me across the finish line. The race wasn't easy, but I think I was grinning from ear to ear the whole race. My kids were at the turn onto the Saginaw Street bricks, and they yelled encouragement. I sprinted to the finish line. I had been told that as first timers crossed the line, their names were announced, so I was waited to hear my name called. Nothing.

I went to pick up my finisher medal and they had run out. Nothing again. I had trained all summer and ran the Crim ten-mile race for what? An apple and a bottle of Dasani?

I sensed someone behind me. Before I could turn around, a medal was being placed over my head and around my neck. When I turned around, there was my best friend, Shari, with no medal around her neck. The Crim brings out the best in people.

Keeley is a good friend and mother of two smaller copies of herself, Chloe, age 11 and Christian, age 8. She is in the Baker College Nursing Program and will graduate in 2006. Running with the Crim Training Program has helped her get through a stressful life change related to divorce. She is one of the smartest people I know and always wins at trivial pursuit. I recommend her as a lifeline if you ever get on a television quiz show.

A Song for the Crim

DARLENE MCKONE

AGE: 66
YEARS WALKING: ABOUT 15
CRIM FINISHES: SEVERAL
YEARS IN CTP: 1
RESIDENCE: GRAND BLANC, MI
OCCUPATION: RETIRED FROM GM 2002

I made up a song for walking group W-7. The only time we sang it in public when we weren't running was at the post-Crim banquet.

This was my first time being involved with any training group. I was hesitant when my friend Wanda Merrill called me to help her, and I must admit there were a few times I wished I hadn't committed myself. I guess we all get a little selfish some time or another. When I was feeling selfish though, I had no idea what my little bit of help meant to so many people, especially to my group.

Anyway, after a few weeks of training, we were running four or five miles, and the group needed something to energize us a bit. We tried singing songs, but as a group we could not find many songs we all knew the words to. So singing popular tunes did not work. This inspired me to come up with an original song. It worked; it really did! At times we sang it two and three times in a night, depending how sluggish we were feeling. Nothing beats the Bradleys like a lively tune. The song is sung to the tune soldiers

march to, a chant called "Sound Off." Running and training was a rewarding experience for me, and I guess I
should have been the one thanking the group instead of
them thanking me!

"Crim Sound Off"

Oh, we don't know but we've been told
The Crim race is for young and old.
Runners, walkers, cyclists, too.
One should be just right for you.

We are walkers, yes, we are.
We have come from near and far.
We're in training for the race.
Hope we can keep up this pace.

Sound Off, one, two
Sound Off, three, four
Sound Off, one, two, three, four.

We may lose a pound or two,
Lower our cholesterol too!
If we don't, we'll still have fun
Walkin', talkin' with everyone.

Up and down these streets and trails
Buildin' up all our morales;
The weather's getting awful hot,
But we still give it all we got.

It gets tougher with each mile.
We don't groan; we just smile,
'cause we're determined, yes, we are
To do ten miles, although it's far!

Sound Off, one, two
Sound Off, three, four
Sound Off, one, two, three, four

Darlene is married and has six children and ten grandchildren. She retired from General Motors after working there for thirty years. She enjoys working out, golfing, bowling, snow skiing, woodcarving, and painting. Most of all, she enjoys spending time with her family.

CRIM FACT:
BY THE 25TH ANNIVERSARY RACE IN 2002,
CRIM CHARITY CONTRIBUTIONS HAD TOTALED
OVER TWO MILLION DOLLARS.

Dis<u>CRIM</u>inating Taste

TODD PAWLIK

Courtesy of brightroom

AGE: 37

YEARS RUNNING: 15

CRIM FINISHES: 13

RESIDENCE: BEVERLY HILLS, MI

OCCUPATION: AUTOMOTIVE ENGINEER

When Sheri and I met in 1992, we each had our own passion. Hers was golf and mine was running. As our relationship developed and it became a certainty that we would eventually become engaged and get married, we decided that each would partake in the other's passion so we could spend more time together. I would learn to golf and Sheri would become a runner.

As a goal for her to aim for, I suggested the 1993 Crim 8K as her first race. I had completed the ten-miler in 1992 and was immediately and forever addicted to the Crim. Sheri trained in the spring and early summer of 1993, increasing her stamina from jogging/walking one mile to entirely jogging five miles. She anxiously awaited her first Crim.

Race day was perfect, at least in my memory. I finished the ten-miler and cheered Sheri as she started the 8K. I then began my second race of the day, this time to the car to retrieve the engagement ring. With ring in hand, I trotted off to the finish line and pleaded with the announcer on the podium to entrust me with the microphone.

I nervously proposed over the loudspeaker system in front of the finish-line crowd as Sheri completed her first Crim 8K. I had intended a romantic, "Sheri, I love you dearly. Will you please marry me?" In my nervous state though, it came out as a less impressive, "Sheri, I was kinda hopin' that you'd marry me." Sheri heard my voice and the proposal, but did not know where I was standing. Luckily, her non-verbal reaction instantly indicated to the crowd and me that she accepted my nervous proposal. I quickly navigated past the unsuspecting finish line officials to Sheri and excitedly placed the ring on her finger. The crowd clapped and cheered its approval in the background.

While maybe not as romantic as proposing on the upper platform of the Eiffel Tower on a warm summer Paris evening, the Crim proposal was a unique, life-changing event that neither Sheri nor I will ever forget. We tell our proposal story often.

The story has a happy ending, too. Sheri and I celebrated our tenth wedding anniversary in 2004. I have completed the Crim ten-mile race every year since 1992. Sheri has adopted running as her passion, runs regularly, and has completed the Crim 8K or 5K almost every year since the proposal in 1993. Every time, she tells me, she hopes for another diamond as she crosses the finish line. Carrying on the family tradition, our four-year-old daughter, Alexandria, and our two-year-old daughter, Rachel, both completed the Teddy Bear Trot in 2004.

The Crim Festival of Races will always have a special place in the hearts and memories of the Pawlik family.

Todd is an automotive engineer from Beverly Hills, Michigan. He and wife Sheri continue to run regularly for fitness, stress relief, and to keep up with young daughters Alexandria and Rachel.

TECHNO GEEK

ANTHONY ELLIS

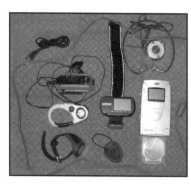

AGE: 41
YEARS RUNNING: 5
CRIM FINISHES: 4
YEARS IN CTP: 4
RESIDENCE: FLUSHING, MI
OCCUPATION: GERIATRIC
  PSYCHIATRIST

When I started running with the Crim Training Program back in 2001, I didn't have the proper equipment for my newfound passion. Now, I'm not talking physically. I didn't have the correct running shoes, clothes, watches, and other technical gadgets. This time was a confusing one for me in my running career as I discovered the scores of different types of running shoes and accessories. I went to Bauman's Running Store, having seen Brian Barkey's welcome lecture to the Crim Training Program.

"Don't get your shoes at the mall. Get them fit by someone who knows what they're doing," he said.

I'd never been in a running store, and I was surprised to find that there were enough products for runners to make up the inventory for a whole store. I thought all I needed were shoes. I saw all the name brand shoes and the prices, as well as the prices for the special moisture-wicking shorts and shirts, and knew I was in trouble.

Having been raised in America and having watched a great deal of television, I ended up with a pair of running shoes with a brand that advertises on television. The shoes had an inspiring, fast-sounding name. I was certain I would break records in them. I bought a pair of black running shorts and a shirt and thought I was ready to go. Little did I know that regular socks frequently cause blisters, especially for beginners. Soon I was back at the store purchasing special socks to protect my fledgling runner's feet, as well as a water carrier belt with room for keys and GU packets. I had to have all the "stuff"; it's my nature. I'm the guy with the entire arsenal of brand-spanking-new equipment for a given sport who then falls, crashes, or otherwise flubs things up. You know the type. They *look* like professional skiers and then fall all over the bunny slope.

Later I found out that to be a real runner, you also had to have a running watch. I experimented with several watches until I found one that had two separate interval timers that could run continuously so that I could set one time as the run time and one as the walk time, using the now-famous Galloway method. The gadget was not enough for me, though. I had the idea that the watch should do more. I wanted a watch that would tell me how fast I was going, how far I had gone, and store plenty of other data that I could analyze later to turn me into a junior Kenyan. I bought a pace watch that worked with a pedometer-like mechanism that was stored in a pod on one of my running shoes. This watch would tell me my current pace, average pace, elapsed time, and beep at a specified distance, such as a one-mile interval. It also had a large face that was slanted in such a way that it was easy to read while running. Boy, was I impressed.

I wore my new watch to all the training group runs and my practice runs and was soon spouting off some of the numbers to the group. Unfortunately, the group members were not as impressed as I had been. Something about saying you've done 1.3 miles when you have six miles to go didn't sit well with folks who were already tired, sweaty, and puffing. I would chime off our pace each mile, and runners told me to shut up.

A couple of other techno geeks were impressed with

the watch and wondered where I had gotten it. Overall, however, I found that most people were interested only in the elapsed time of the run, and could have gotten that information from their own $19.95 bargain special. The fact that my watch provided seven times more information was partially offset by the fact that it cost seven times the price.

The watch proved useful to me in my training, and I became dependent on it. Unfortunately, the battery in the foot pod had a nasty habit of going dead right in the middle of a crucial race, leaving me data-less, clueless, and demoralized. I was eventually freed from my dependence on the watch when I forgot to take it to a race and didn't have enough time to go back home and get it. It was one of the local evening 5K races, and I actually ran faster without the watch, much to my chagrin. That bit of data was lost on me, however, as I continued to pursue other technical gadgets to enhance the running experience.

I purchased an MP3 player, which is a device that allows me to take songs from CDs or the Internet and store them in a small, lightweight device that I can listen to while running. The MP3 became my next junior obsession. I created specific groups of songs for individual races and goal times. I found there was nothing like a bit of punchy, hard-driving music to boost mid-race performance. Over time I outgrew my first MP3 player, which was an archaic model that used a small hard drive that I bounced to death. I moved on to models that were indestructible and easier to use. My most recent iteration of the MP3 player is smaller and lighter and quite a technical wonder...when I can find it.

An unfortunate side effect of wearing an MP3 player during a race is that people complain that the runner's are not fully aware of what's going on around them and can't tell when it's safe to change lanes. For me awareness actually is an issue, because more people pass me than vice versa, and I need to know where they are when they're going around me and leaving me in the dust. I have tried to work around this problem by staying out of other people's way in general and trying not to start too far forward in the pack at the beginning of a race. I'm in the group of runners who are dependent on their technical gadgets and music to complement the overall running experience.

My fascination with technological gadgets continues, and last year I purchased a global positioning system pace watch for my wife for Mother's Day. It stores all sorts of running information. It has a training log and is quite an amazing little device. It's really a small computer, and it's somewhat complicated to use. My wife tried it twice, donated it back to me, and implied that I had known she wouldn't be able to use it and planned to use it myself the whole time.

Even though I was taken aback with her critical view of my gift-picking skills, I have made up for it by offering my skills as a foot masseuse for her tired toes after long runs. Who else but an absolutely dedicated spouse is going to touch the feet of a runner after those feet have been in running shoes for ten-miles? Perhaps next year I will get her a complicated MP3 player.

Riley, Why Do You Do It?

RILEY MCLINCHA

Courtesy of Marathon Foto

AGE: 54
YEARS RUNNING: 29
CRIM FINISHES: ALL 28
YEARS IN CTP: 5
RESIDENCE: CLIO, MI
OCCUPATION: ENTERTAINER,
  RETIRED GM TRADESMAN

Are you a veteran Crim runner whose times are getting slower? Do you feel that it's not as much fun as it used to be? Are you thinking about throwing in the towel saying, "No more Crims for me?" Stop...Don't quit! Walk it, if you have to. It's not about the time. All runners who cross the finish line are winners. I know it sounds like a lame cliché, but it is true. It's time to stop being serious. Hey, you might find a way of making it more fun.

To many area runners, the Crim is the race they peak for each year. So it was for me, the first ten years of its existence. Although I wouldn't admit it then, I was way too serious, like the year I set my PR of 64:59.9. I wanted to break sixty-five minutes. You can't get any closer than that. It almost came at a terrible cost. I was dehydrated to the extent that I do not remember anything about the last mile. The first person to my aid was my father. "Dad, get me something to drink," I said, frothing at the mouth. He grabbed the first thing he saw in a cup and handed it to me. I was so thirsty I might have drunk gasoline if it was handed to me. I gulped it down, and it was beer. Back then runners were served beer right on Saginaw Street. Its effect hit me almost immediately. I leaned backwards against a building and slid down to the sidewalk.

When my wife and daughters found me, they asked, "What's wrong with him?"

"I think he's drunk," Dad told them.

I did rehydrate with proper liquids, and as you can tell, I lived. Needless to say getting beer out of the chute area and onto the flat lot was a wise move.

I continued my Crim PR quest in years to follow, always praying for cool weather and no heavy rain, then along came 1986, the year of the Crim Swim. The torrential downpour left some places of the course under water. Unlike the nine previous Crims, I arrived at this race alone. The morning of the race my family and I arrived home at 4:00 a.m. from Metro Airport after picking up an exchange student. I had only an hour of sleep before I put a bicycle in the van and drove to the race. I chained up the bike near the finish line and drove to the start at Mott Community College.

The race began as usual, but rain soon moved in...no, a *monsoon* moved in. Curbsides turned into creeks, and running shoes turned into anvils. When I finished I was so disappointed that I didn't break seventy minutes that I did not join in the festivities. I unchained my bike, rode back to my van, and went home.

I told my wife about what happened, and she asked, "Well, didn't you talk to your dad at the finish?"

In my selfish moment of pity I had forgotten my father and left him wandering the downtown finish area looking for me. He was seventy-five years old and did not get around that well, but like every prior year, he made the effort to meet the family downtown to watch the Crim. I drove back to Flint and looked for him, but by then he had given up and gone home. I've always regretted abandoning the man that was always there to give me kudos for my efforts. He would be around for just three more Crims, and I made the most of them. As soon as I finished I found my number-one fan. Together we enjoyed the festivities until *he* was exhausted.

In the days following the Crim Swim the idea kept returning to my head that I was taking the race *way* too seriously, but I knew I would be red-lining the course again the next year, unless I changed my focus. The centipede crossed my mind, and I wished I could run with it which would take my focus off speed. The centipede was a group of runners that in the early days of the Crim ran as one unit, single file, with decorated bed sheets over them and only their heads sticking out. They always had fun and were a crowd favorite.

I also had a running gimmick, but did it only when no one was watching. I was a closet "joggler," something I tried after reading about it in a running magazine. I'd carry juggling balls with me on training runs, and when cars and houses were out of sight, I'd juggle. It was my form of fartlek running.

The fall that followed the Crim Swim I was caught joggling by fellow runners John Gault, Ken, and daughter Kelly Shumate. I was slightly embarrassed but got positive feedback. "Now there's a happy-go-lucky runner," Ken said and laughed. I was out of the closet, and a light bulb went on in my head. I knew what I'd do in next year's Crim.

I showed up the following August with what looked like real eggs, but they were actually plastic. I found the centipede. It was quite small, only three runners, and I shook their hands. It turned out to be the centipede's last year. Previously they group had as many as ten runners, but over the years the number dwindled. The following year, 1988, they did not appear at all; its member's handshakes turned out to be a passing of the Crim-jester torch.

The joggling of the Crim came off without a hitch. I

got positive feedback from spectators and other runners, but more importantly I had more fun, because I wasn't trying to kill myself. I continued the joggling thing for six more Crims. I took it a notch higher with the development of *drubbling,* which involved dribbling three basketballs while I ran. It caught the attention of more ears and eyes because of the drumming sound and higher visibility. With even more positive responses, I had found my new niche. I admit I do get rare negative reactions, not usually from runners who don't like being beaten by a runner dribbling three basketballs, but more often from people who dislike the annoying noise it creates. I rationalize those complaints, at least to myself, knowing drubbling has raised more than $12,000 for cancer research, in addition to the amount it has raised for Special Olympics.

I sometimes get asked if I ever get the urge to run the Crim without the basketballs. It crosses my mind, but I run the course throughout the year and pretty much know what my time would be for any given Crim. I also run enough other races seriously and my competition knows what I could do in the Crim if I sought glory again. As usual, I would not place in my age group.

I still miss the centipede. I wish someone would resurrect the old worm. I'd organize it myself, but too many spectators expect to see the "The Basketball Dude." Somebody please revive it! You won't regret it. Whatever gimmicks you come up with, remember safety comes first. Follow the rules and go to the back of the pack. If you feel the urge to get closer to the starting line, you're still too serious. Your time still matters to you. Wait another year or two. Most importantly, keep your Crim string alive. If you can't run, walk. If you can't walk, use crutches or a wheelchair.

For me, Riley started out as the guy who runs while bouncing three basketballs. He routinely crossed the finish line before me in my first two years of running despite his signature basketball maneuvers. He is much more than a

Crim race jester to his friends and the Flint running scene. I had the pleasure of hearing him sing "The Star Spangled Banner," quite well I thought, at the beginning of a local 5K where I set a personal best. His rendition inspired me, but I was still barely edged out by an eight-year-old at the finish.

You can find the words to Riley's "Spirit of the Crim" anthem in the appendix of this book, and on his CD titled, "Life of Riley."

CRIM FACT:
THE 178 INTERSECTIONS ARE STAFFED
BY MORE THAN 500 VOLUNTEERS.

Images from the Crim

Friday night's pasta party gets you ready to tackle the Saturday morning races.

Crim start line preparations are being made for race day. The blue line that marks the course route and the start and finish line areas needs to be repainted each year.

Former race director Sherlynn Everly (left) at a pre-race VIP event, 2001.

Michigan Special Olympics and the Crim Festival of Races make a great team.

The Crim Sports and Fitness Expo starts the Thursday before race weekend. This is where runners pick up their race packets and look over the newest running shoes, clothes, supplements, and local health and fitness services.

Local running stores support the Crim and vice versa. Runners find time for some last-minute shopping during the Expo, and expect some good deals from Curtis.

(courtesy of Marathon Foto)

Local medical centers and other health and service organizations are on hand at the pre-race expo showing their support for the Crim Festival of Races.

Various local corporations support the Crim and field teams for the big race. It's a great way to invest in the health of employees and develop corporate pride.

The Crim Training Program prepares groups of Crim hopefuls. Dorie (far left) and Brian Barkey (bottom right) are integral to the success of the program, as are the other volunteer group leaders and Crim staff.

The Galloway Run/Walk method produces hundreds of personal success stories on race day through the Crim Training Program.

Olympian, author, and running coach, Jeff Galloway, welcomes new runners and spreads the word on how to enjoy running and avoid injuries.

Jeff Galloway signs Crim posters at the Galloway running clinic and picnic in 2003.

The Galloway picnic provides pizza, posters, and wisdom for attendees.

Smiling Galloway picnic goers having fun with other runners.

Crim Training Program, 2001.

Crim Training Program, 2003.

Runner start, 2001.

Wheeler start, 2001.

Bring it on!

The Kenyan lead group runs up the first of the three dreaded Bradley hills. These hills at the five-mile marker take a toll on mid-race morale, but add to the challenge.

(courtesy of Marathon Foto)

"Catherine the Great" Ndereba wins again in 2000. The people of Flint know and love Catherine, a six-time Crim winner. It was especially gratifying to see her go on to win the silver medal at the Athens Olympics in 2004.

(courtesy of Marathon Foto)

The bricks of Saginaw Street take Crim participants to this sweet sight.

Brian Barkey leads another group to Crim glory.

Anyone can "see" the Crim finish line with help.

Finish-line volunteers help with water, fruit, frozen treats, and hand out the medals.
Runners who need help are directed to first-aid stations.

Finish-line socializing usually includes a mile-by-mile analysis, congratulations, and talk of next years race goal, followed by a trip to the beer and food tent. The post-race entertainment is always first-rate.

Race day 2001—the start of a family tradition.

(courtesy of Marathon Foto)

Crim Festival of Races, 1998.

Walkers are welcome at the Crim.

Welcoming a new Crimster with a quilt of race shirts.

Hey look Mom, I'm a runner too!

Future Crim ten-milers participate in a group of events just for kids.

A helping hand from Mom is all it takes.

Crim Kids Classic, 2002.

I'm gonna get a medal like Mom's!

Teddy Bear Trot, 2000.

My little Crimster waits for the start, as her Grandma looks on from the far right.

Hey, who owns these?

Chloe and Rosalyn having fun at the Crim Kids Classic in 2004.

We are the champions...

Keeley and Christian Byerly run the one-mile event.

Just clowning around at the Crim Kids Classic.

A high five from a friend pumps up the fun.

Swartz Creek Marching Band.

Crim staff sell race souvenirs at merchandise tables.

Crim triumph! Brian and Shirin celebrate at the end of the race.

The five pages that follow contain the Crim T-shirt artwork from 1977 to 2004. These images were obtained by photographing a complete Crim T-shirt collection owned by Wally McLaughlin, a CTP group leader, and Crim story contributor. The collection has been on display several times in Flint, and is the only one of its kind. The collection illustrates the history of the Bobby Crim 10 Mile Road Race for Special Olympics as the race has grown in size and changed in name during the last twenty-eight years. Thank you Wally for your interest and generosity.

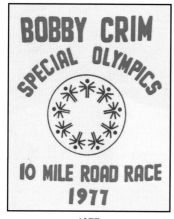

1977

1978

1979

1980

1981

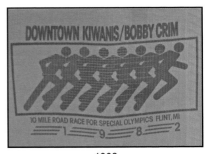

1982

1983

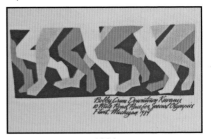

1984

1985

1986

1987

1988

1989

1990

1991

1992

1993

1994

1995

1996

1997

1998

1999

2000

2001

2002

2003

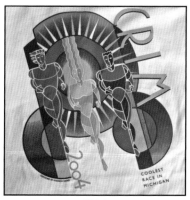

2004

CHAPTER FIVE

Obstacles Overcome

WE ARE RUNNING TOGETHER

SHIRIN B. MANZARI

AGE: 57
YEARS RUNNING: 7
CRIM FINISHES: 6
YEARS IN CTP: 5
RESIDENCE: FLINT, MI
OCCUPATION: IVF LAB,
    HURLEY MEDICAL CENTER

I started to run the Crim in 1999 because of my son Shahin. He was twenty-six years old, and had graduated as an electrical engineer from Kettering University. He had also taken and passed the admissions test for medical school.

Shahin signed up for the Crim in 1995. He was excited and motivated. Every day he ran to get ready for the Crim race. Unfortunately, on July 17, 1995, Shahin was diagnosed with a very rare cancer called "sarcoma." A few weeks later, after tests were done at the University of Michigan in Ann Arbor, it was found that the cancer had metastasized to his bones. His doctors advised him to avoid strenuous activities, especially running.

Shahin was a strong young man, and he was in good shape. Seldom sick in his life, he couldn't believe what had happened to him. He tried to convince his doctor that he had no problems when he was running, but he was told his problem was serious, and he would have to stop running. He had tears in his eyes when he heard the bad news.

It hurt me to see my young son become so disappointed and sad. Sometimes he cried. I had never seen him cry, since his childhood. It made me sad and upset whenever he cried over his cancer. I did not know what to say. I would just say, "I know you will be fine." I had no doubt he would be fine. I couldn't describe my feelings at that time, being a mother of a son with cancer.

I assured him all the time, "You will be fine after the treatments. We will run together." I promised him.

He was not a little boy. I don't know why I told him "We will run together." I still don't know. I really thought we would. At that time, I was forty-seven years old and had never run in my life. I couldn't even walk more than one-half mile. How those words came to my mouth, I still don't know.

Shahin started his treatment. He stopped all his activities and running. He decided to be strong and have a good attitude to fight against his cancer.

He asked me, "I need your help, Mother." He continued, "I could make it with your help."

I replied, "My son, you know me very well; I work hard, and we can do it together with God's help."

His doctors and nurses told us several times, "Shahin is one of the strongest patients we have ever had before." They had a strong belief that he could fight the cancer.

Shahin had a sense of humor. Once in a while, he teased me about what I said to him, about our running together.

He asked me with a smile, "Are you sure you will run with me?"

Unfortunately, after two years of struggling and working hard together with my husband and daughter's support, Shahin didn't make it. We lost him on February 22, 1997.

I became sad and depressed. I was almost handicapped after he left me for good. I couldn't go back to normal life. I could not work. I quit school. I was going to Mott

College when he got sick and stopped going to help him to fight his cancer. My life had changed completely. I had no hope. I had no power to comfort my husband and my daughter. I put on weight. I didn't care about the way I looked. My changes felt very bad and were not like me, which made my daughter unhappy and disappointed.

She was twenty-two years old at that time. She and Shahin had been close. She became lonely after losing Shahin. People knew us as a happy family before that tragedy changed our lives. The new situation made my daughter and my husband very sad. We were not a happy family anymore.

Finally my daughter talked to me seriously. She wanted me to go back to a normal life and back to school and work. She reminded me what I had promised my son, "We will run together." I knew it was not fair what I was doing to my family. She was my child, too. She lost her brother, and she was losing me as well. I asked God, "Please help me handle this job and turn my family in the right direction."

I thought, "For running, I need to walk first for a while." I found out later that I was right. I started to walk, and after about a month, I gradually began to run. One year later, in February 1998, I had been running by myself for one year. In August 1999, I ran the Crim for five miles.

Since 1999, every year, I have run the whole ten miles in the Crim. This year is the sixth year I have run in the Crim. I am proud of myself. I am running for my son. Every time I go up the Bradley hills, when I pass his old apartment, I call his name out loud and say: "Shahin, my love! I am running for you! I love you. We are running together."

Shirin's husband Saeed, and son Shahin, immigrated to the United States from Iran in 1984. The two worked in a printing shop together and later opened up their own printing business. This was quite a change from Saeed's former job as a helicopter pilot in Iran. Shirin and her daughter, Shadi moved to the U.S. a year later, in 1985. Shirin and her family placed a high emphasis on education and hard work. Her son Shahin became an electrical engineer and was working in that capacity when he became ill. Her daughter Shadi graduated from Columbia University in May 2005 with a degree in physical therapy. Shirin has trained as a certified nurse assistant, dental assistant, medical secretary and health unit coordinator and works at Hurley Medical Center.

Shirin's ability to describe how she found meaning in her family tragedy is a triumphant example of the strength of the human spirit. I was lucky enough to be present when Shirin told this story in person at a Crim Training Program celebration banquet. My wife got the idea to collect these stories and put them in a book after she heard Shirin. It takes tremendous courage to bear witness to your pain for the benefit of others. This story is my favorite one about running through pain to get to the other side.

PLANES, PAINS, AND AUTOMOBILES

ALLISON ENSIGN

AGE: 34
YEARS RUNNING: 30
CRIM FINISHES: 10
RESIDENCE: FENTON, MI
OCCUPATION: FULL-TIME MOTHER OF FIVE

I am a thirty-four-year-old mother of five children, which is probably my proudest accomplishment. My next would have to be that on August 28, 2004, I finished my tenth consecutive Crim ten-mile race. Ten Crims may not seem like a huge accomplishment to some people, but wait. It's the consecutive part amid great obstacles that gets interesting.

I am a native Michigander; however, I haven't lived in Michigan all my life. For three of my Crim races I was a resident of Tooele, Utah. Those years I altered schedules and caught a plane East to Michigan for the late August race each year.

In August 1999, I was seated on a flight next to several Kenyans who spoke very little English. I was able to communicate with them enough to find out that they were, in fact, flying into Flint to compete in the Crim, too. No doubt they had higher expectations for their efforts, but it was exciting to pretend for a brief moment that we were all equals flying in for the same competition. I had run in the event more times than any of them which seemed to impress them. I didn't want to ruin their image of me, so I never told them my pace and how they are finishing when I'm barely more than halfway through.

When we arrived at Bishop Airport, the people who were supposed to meet the visitors were not there. Because of culture and language barriers, the Kenyans were confused and looked lost. I was able to make a few phone calls and find the host hotel and someone who was in charge of taking care of the Kenyans. They were glad to hear from me and learn that their star racers were found. They were appreciative, and it was my pleasure to get the stars to the Crim safely. Like most runners of the Crim, I never saw the Kenyans again. Well, that is, unless you count me watching them run in the front pack on the PBS television coverage later that evening.

Running isn't my only hobby. I am also a black belt in Tae Kwon Do. In August 2001, I was doing a jump kick and landed slightly harder than usual on my right leg. I felt an excruciating pain as my calf muscle tore about four inches. The never-before experienced sensation of feeling a muscle tear was worse than the pain. It reminded me of the feel of ripping a chicken breast off the breastbone. I was unable to put any weight at all on my right leg for about a week and a half. After that I was able to limp along with a cane, being careful not to injure it further. Did a torn muscle stop me from running the ten-mile race? No way, not the Crim. I limped to the start line and received several strange looks from runners and spectators as well. Needless to say, I didn't get a personal best that year, but that's not the important thing. Perseverance combined with a fairly high dose of ibuprofen helped me overcome my injury and continue my streak of consecutive entries.

You might think if those obstacles didn't stop me nothing would. My biggest challenge has been recovering quickly enough from childbirth to run ten miles. Two of my five children were born before my first Crim. Three were born during the ten-year span. My son Luke was born May 24, 2001, leaving me three months to get in shape. In

1998, my son Jack was born June 30, leaving me less than two months to get in shape; but wait, it gets worse. This year my son Jonah came July 14, leaving me six weeks to get in shape. For those of you unfamiliar with recovering from childbirth, doctors recommend waiting eight weeks before resuming an exercise program. I didn't tell the doctor at my eight-week postpartum exam that I had done several eight-mile runs at just four or five weeks postpartum to train for the Crim. It's our secret.

Why, you may wonder? Why spend thousands of dollars on plane fares, when you have no chance of winning prize money? Why run on an injured calf muscle and risk further damage, pain, and a lengthier recovery time? Why risk my personal health by jump-starting exercise so soon after having babies? I'll tell you why. The Crim is not just the "Coolest race in Michigan." In my book, it is *the* Coolest Race, period. It has become part of my heart. How long will I keep up my consecutive streak? My goal is fifty consecutive years. I'll check back with you in 2044 and fill you in!

Allison is a 1987 graduate of Fenton High School. She completed a degree in Broadcast Journalism at Brigham Young University in Provo, Utah in 1992. She holds a black belt in Tae Kwon Do. In addition to running, Allison enjoys reading, and vacationing with her family. She has finished the Crim ten consecutive times and hopes to keep her streak alive for many years.

CRIM WHEELERS: A PROUD HISTORY

In 1979 Bill Sills was the first wheelchair athlete to compete in a major racing event anywhere. His racing debut was the Crim ten-mile road race, and he finished with a time of 1:53:54.

Jimbo Boyd helped expand the wheeler participation in 1981. Kris Lenzo finished the Crim course with an astounding time of 49:32. Pat Ford became the first female wheeler entrant.

In 1987, Jim Martinson, the world-record holder in the 10K, completed the Crim ten-mile course in 49:14, despite finishing with a flat tire. In the same year Russ Monroe led quadriplegic participants with a time of 58:30 and moved on to world competition.

In 1990 McLaren Regional Rehabilitation Center became the Wheeler Division sponsor. Scott Holenbeck set the Crim course record, winning the Para class in 41:46. Brad White of Flushing finished a close second in 42:00 minutes. Candace Cable made her first Flint appearance, finishing first with a time of 46:35.

In 1991 the Crim hosted the biggest wheeler division ever, starting forty-two wheelchair athletes. The University of Illinois' elite wheeling team participated, enhancing the competitive field with nationally known wheelchair athletes.

We did not receive any stories from wheelers, but did not want to leave them out.

CURRENT CRIM COURSE RECORDS

OPEN MEN 45:43

OPEN WOMEN 51.47

MASTER MEN . . . . 47:25 CR & WR

MASTER WOMEN 54:46

WHEELER MEN . . . . 35:18 CR & WR

WHEELER WOMEN 43:20

Submitted by the Crim Organization

CRIM FACT:

FOR THE FIRST TIME IN CRIM HISTORY, HAND CRANK WHEELCHAIR RACERS PARTICIPATED IN 2004.

A Sister's Inspiration

RICH STOOLMAKER

RICH

AGE: 45
YEARS RUNNING: 20
CRIM FINISHES: 17
RESIDENCE: FENTON, MI
OCCUPATION: ELECTRONICS ENGINEER

REGINA

This is the third year that my sister Regina has participated in the Crim. She has had many challenges to overcome since she was an unsuspecting passenger in a terrible car accident that took four young lives. She spent ninety-nine days at St. Mary Hospital in Saginaw and another seventy-nine days at Hurley Medical Center in Flint, Michigan.

For the first year after the accident, she remained close to the health care system with rehab treatments and many visits to the doctor. For most of her stay at St. Mary, she was in such critical condition that I, as her brother, could do nothing. I felt useless and came to understand how illness changes the little control we have over our lives.

After my sister improved, I was able to help more over time. Time went on, and a trust developed between her health care providers and me. They let me do more and more for her, and by the time she was ready for rehab, I was included on her "treatment team." I have been by her side ever since to try to make her life better.

We were told early on that because of the severity of her injuries, which included a traumatic brain injury, we should not set our goals for her too high. Doctors said it would be good if she one day got out of bed and into a wheelchair. I knew she was going to do much better than that. Her spirit is much too strong to hold down. Because of her spirit, she has overcome a great deal and sets a standard we can all learn from.

Almost everyone knows Regina at the Hurley Health and Fitness Center. They know how she pushes herself, and they know her spirit can rub off on them.

Although she required some assistance to maintain her balance, she finished the one-mile walk in a personal record time of thirty-seven minutes. The walk was difficult for her, and I could see it in her face. I asked her at the three-quarter mile mark if she was OK.

She said, "Yes, it's all about coming down the red bricks."

As we made our way down Saginaw, the people on the sidelines clapped. They saw her determination, they felt her energy and spirit, and we felt their good wishes reflecting back. The absolute goodness that the Crim brings to Flint is part of the same spirit we felt as we came down to the finish.

She collapsed in her chair from the effort and said with the energy she had left, "If I can do it, there is no reason any of you standing can't do it."

Thank you for supporting the Crim and thanks to all of the people who make it happen.

Rich has been running for twenty years because its a part of who he is. He has assisted his sister, Regina, over the past nine years during her arduous recovery from a tragic auto accident. Regina works to help others and volunteers in local schools. She also volunteers for The Children's Miracle Network. Although she needs some help with her balance and gets fatigued easily, she has been walking the one-mile Crim race since the year 2000. Rich hopes Regina will someday complete the ten-mile Crim.

BLESSINGS IN DISGUISE

KAREN DANIELS WOLBERT

Courtesy of brightroom

AGE: 46
YEARS RUNNING: 13
CRIM FINISHES: 6
YEARS IN CTP: 2
RESIDENCE: FLINT, MI
OCCUPATION: PHYSICAL EDUCATION TEACHER

My relationship with the Crim started seventeen years ago. My children were very young then. We used to sit out on our porch and watch the runners go by. Our preparation included getting supplies of coffee, doughnuts and milk, after which we settled in for some serious spectating. It was always so exciting to see some strugglers and some other runners just glide by.

After the last runner, I would always tell my kids, "I'm going to be in that race next year!" They usually had a good laugh over that prediction.

Well, that year finally did arrive in 1996. I joined the Crim Training Program and with their help, I did it. I ran the ten-mile race. I was slow, but it didn't matter. I finished. As long as I ran over "the bricks", it counted. I ran the Crim again for the next few years until I got some bad news about my health.

On a dreadful day in March of 2001, I was told that I had brain cancer and it would be difficult to remove. I was totally devastated when I heard those words. My brother-in-law died from a brain tumor three years prior to my diagnosis. Coming after that family loss, my news was very difficult for everyone. The cancer turned me into a spectator again, but I was determined not to let it control me and my life!

I went to quite a few different hospitals to hear what other surgeons had to say. I was scheduled for surgery at two different hospitals and wasn't sure which one I wanted for the surgery. My second son knew I wasn't sure which hospital, but one day he went to a Mass that was being said for me, and the priest kept talking of the providence of the Lord. Providence Hospital was one of the hospitals I was considering, so, I figured with his faith, how could I go anywhere else? I went to Providence Hospital and was blessed with a wonderful surgeon and began my treatment and recovery.

Getting my strength back was difficult, but I was given another blessing, a wonderful family and friends who came over and took me for walks. Slowly, a block turned into two blocks, and so on until one day I realized I had walked a mile. I decided I would walk every day and try to get my strength back. I always enjoyed walking, but I missed the way I used to feel after a good run.

I am a physical education teacher, so when I returned to teaching, I wanted to prove to the students that I was okay. I wanted to show them that cancer isn't always a death sentence. They knew it could sometimes be embarrassing to live with. One day in class while I was teaching the kids to shoot a basketball, the ball hit me in the head, and my wig went flying off! The kids weren't sure what to think. Thank God for a nearby colleague's intervention. She explained to the kids what happened, while I recovered from the wig shot.

In the past, I had a little cross country camp to get kids ready for the Turkey Trot. I didn't want to let the kids down, so I thought I might try running again. I did, and amazingly, here I am! I am anxious, afraid, and slow, but nothing will give me greater pleasure than to wear my Crim shirt to school and know that I am still alive. My family is really proud of me for attempting to run the Crim this year. We have come a long way from sitting with our doughnuts and just watching. My two older children were going to run the ten-mile race, but instead all three will be cheering me on. Another blessing.

Karen told me "I started out slow and I'm still slow, but at least I'm out there". She is a P.E. teacher setting a good example for her students. She is also the mother of "three wonderful human beings" whom she thinks of as kids, but added, "they are all grown ups!"

CRIM FACT:
IN 2004, THE CRIM FESTIVAL OF RACES DREW
A TOTAL OF 13,744 PARTICIPANTS.

ONCE UPON A SUMMER

DEB KIERTZNER

AGE: 39 AND HOLDING
YEARS RUNNING: 5
CRIM FINISHES: 3
YEARS IN CTP: 3
RESIDENCE: FLUSHING, MI
OCCUPATION: CRIM RACE DIRECTOR

*As told to Training Program partici-
pants at 2005 orientation.*

In the spring of 2000 I received the diagnosis of cancer. My treatment included major surgery, a life-changing
experience. Following the successful surgery, treatments,
and brief recovery period, I needed a way to regain my
health. I wanted to get back in shape, build up my morale,
and keep the cancer at bay.

A friend suggested the Crim Training Program as a
way to achieve those goals, and we joined in the spring of
2003. We signed up for the walking program and went to
the orientation. We started the beginners program and
attended all the information sessions. My group, my friend,
and I enjoyed ourselves every week.

A few weeks into the summer, my long-standing
friend Dorie Barkey suggested we should consider moving
up into the running program. I was never a runner, and
the idea of training to run the Crim was, in my opinion,
something other people did. In fact, when I told my family

what I was considering, they thought I had lost my mind. My daughters couldn't comprehend it. I was over forty, recovering from cancer, and had never run a day in my life. When I went home and casually announced over dinner that I was going to run the Crim, my 11-year-old daughter suggested that perhaps the surgeons had removed a good portion of my brain along with my ovaries.

Yes, I think I provided a great deal of humor for them that spring, pouring over my Jeff Galloway book nightly, visiting Bauman's Running Store to be fitted for the perfect running shoes, tearing out down the driveway each evening to run my ever-advancing distance, but I am here to tell you about having the last laugh that summer.

My friend and I did move up into the running program. We faithfully showed up every Tuesday and followed the instructions and words of wisdom from our wonderful group leaders. We were a husband-and-wife team with boundless enthusiasm for the program. We were also blessed with a friendly, funny, and supportive running group.

When I look back I remember much about that summer with fondness. We met some Tuesdays at St. John Vianney Church and ran up Chevrolet Avenue, past the 1920 GM bungalows, fading reminders of Flint's glory days as a booming factory town. We met some weeks at Kettering University and ran down Sunset to Third Avenue, crossing the river and passing the golf course, chatting it up with the golf-cart riders easing their way up the fairways. We met behind Hurley Health and Fitness Center and ran through the older Flint neighborhoods east of Dort Highway. Those runs took us past the few remaining bars and honky-tonks once frequented by the 1930s "Sit Downers" from Flint's labor-organizing past. We ran through the beautiful Court Street neighborhoods and past the stately homes off Miller Road. The Crim course really does show the history of Flint, Michigan. What a perfect way to get a renewed perspective on the Flint community.

As we ran we learned new phrases, like "car back" and "car front" and "White Horse Tavern at 7:30!" That first summer was an emotional re-entry into life after cancer. We grew stronger and faster and more confident. How proud we were the first night we successfully ran up and down the dreaded Bradley hills! What I remember most about that summer, though, was walking *and running* the entire 8K race from start to finish, all the way across the finish line on August 24, 2002.

To all you running rookies out there, this is spring training. A fabulous summer season waits for you, and I am here to tell you that whichever race you are in, whether it is the ten-mile race or the 5K, and whether you walk or run, when you pass the finish line, you will feel like you hit a grand slam in the seventh game of the World Series. That feeling and what you learn your first summer running will remain with you for a very long time.

Good luck with your program!!

CHAPTER SIX
I've Lost Part of Myself

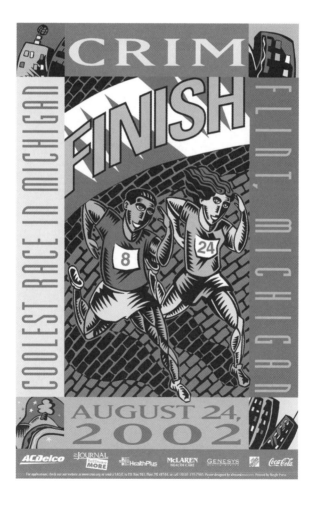

MIRACULOUS TRANSFORMATION

TAMARA SAVAGE

BEFORE

AFTER

AGE: 51

YEARS RUNNING: 2

CRIM FINISHES: 2

YEARS IN CTP: 2

RESIDENCE: SWARTZ CREEK, MI

OCCUPATION: HURLEY HEALTH
SERVICES, VICE PRESIDENT

I watched in awe as the runners finished the ten-mile Crim Festival of Races in August 1999. The focus of my admiration wasn't the Kenyans John Korir and Catherine Ndereba, who finished the race in 46:54 and 54:21 respectively. Instead, my eyes were drawn to the forty-something runners who were finishing in two hours. What excited me was that they looked like regular people. Even more striking was the look of pride and accomplishment on their faces as they grinned their way down the finishers' chute. People around me talked about how those people started running through the Crim Training Program. I made a silent vow that I would get back in shape and participate in the Crim Training Program some day.

By 1999, I was looking forward to my forty-sixth birthday. I had been smoking for thirty years. Although I'd

been active in sports in high school and had continued playing softball until my early forties, having a full-time career and being the single parent of two sons dominated my time. As a lifetime member of Weight Watchers, I knew what I should eat, but soccer games, basketball games, laundry, shopping, yard work, and helping with homework made bad eating choices seem justified. My weight increased from 140 pounds in 1989 to 200 pounds by 1999.

Running the Crim stayed mostly in the back of my mind, but in October 2000, as I approached my forty-eighth birthday, I decided to take control of my life and become fit by fifty. To me, that meant running the Crim race. I knew I needed a plan. Being organized and planning was something I did routinely in my role as Vice President of Hurley Health Services. I laid out an eighteen-month plan to guide me.

Step one of the plan was to quit smoking, in February 2002, eighteen months before my fiftieth birthday, I smoked my last cigarette. I'd tried to quit several times before, but always started smoking again. This time, however, I was determined to run the Crim and be fit by fifty, so the cigarettes stayed in the trash can.

Step two was to rejoin Weight Watchers, which I did in October 2002, two weeks before my forty-ninth birthday. By then, quitting smoking had added another thirty-three pounds and had pushed me to an all-time high weight of 233 pounds. I also joined Curves for Women two weeks later as a way to establish a baseline fitness level.

Step three was to sign up for the Crim Training Program in April 2003. A friend persuaded me to sign up for the ten-mile training, but I knew I'd be happy if I could make it through the 5K race. By the start of training, I'd lost forty-seven pounds, but I wondered how I could possibly run at 186 pounds. The first night of Crim training was a life-changing event. Several speakers and more than 500 Crim Training Program participants were in the room, but the speaker who seemed to talk directly to me was Brian Barkey. I was sure he was at least as old as I was! More importantly, he promised each of us that we could finish the program and achieve the goal of running the Crim ten-mile race. He explained that we would be following a program developed by Jeff Galloway. He said that based on our fitness and speed, we would be divided into groups of twenty. The beginner groups would train by running for two minutes, slowly, and then walking for two minutes. Over the fifteen-week program, we would gradually increase our mileage until we could run/walk ten-miles. Unbelievable!

We headed outside to run a mile so we could be placed in our groups. As I neared the finish line, I saw my good friend Ann Thibodeau waiting for me. Although she was a much faster runner, she waited for me, so she could be in my Crim Training Group to offer encouragement.

During the next fifteen weeks, I marveled at the patience and good humor of our group leaders, Martha Hosmer-Arion and Randy Wilson. Randy was a much faster runner, but he seemed content to go at our pace and offer us encouragement. At first it was a struggle to run for the whole two minutes, but Martha, Randy, and Ann encouraged me with every step. I did every bit of homework assigned, running shorter runs two other days of the week and walking most non-running days. By the beginning of July 2003, I'd lost twenty more pounds and was down to 165 pounds.

By race day on August 23, 2003, I'd lost a total of seventy-six pounds and weighed in at 157 pounds. I was so excited about the race that I didn't sleep much the night before. Halfway to the race, I realized I needed to turn around and go back home because I didn't have my watch. How can you be a "Gallowalker" (a name people call those that adhere to Jeff Galloway's run/walk philosophy) if you don't know when to run and when to walk? When I finally got to the starting area, I was overwhelmed when the national anthem started. Suddenly, my nervousness left me. I knew that the Crim Training Program had prepared me for the challenge ahead. Slightly more than two hours later, I achieved my goal! My running partner and I held our linked hands far above our heads as we crossed the finish line. "Fit by fifty" was no longer a goal, it was a reality.

The year since my first Crim has been a busy one. I run four days a week with various running groups, and I lift weights at the YMCA two days a week. In January 2004, I signed up for the Leukemia and Lymphoma Society's Team In Training Program with my buddy Ann Thibodeau. We each raised more than $1,500 for Team in Training as we trained for, and ultimately ran, the Bayshore Marathon in May 2004. We also signed up as Crim group leaders and trained with the "Marvelous" Group M. It was fulfilling for me to be able to give back just a little bit to the program that had made such a remarkable change in my life.

I recently weighed in at 133 pounds, a total of 100 pounds lighter than two years ago. I have completed three marathons and plan to begin training for an ultra marathon (50K or more) in January 2005. My doctor recently told me that with a body fat percentage of 17.8, I needed to put on a few pounds. I never thought I'd live to hear a physician tell me that! And to think, it all started with watching the Crim Road Race five years ago. The most remarkable thing about my adventure isn't the weight loss or fitness I achieved, it's the wonderful and supportive running friends I've made who continue to encourage me with every step I take.

Tamara works at Hurley Health Services as a Vice President. She has taken on running with a passion. Since starting the Crim Training Program in May 2003 as part of getting "Fit by Fifty", Tamara completed the Crim in August 2003, a half-marathon in October 2003, and then her first marathon in May 2004. In the last year, she has completed four more marathons, and is the first person I know of from the training group to go on to Ultra-marathons (any distance longer than a marathon). Her first ultra will be a fifty mile race on July 2, 2005. Her ultimate goal is "Fifty Times Two by Fifty-Two". Translated, that means she wants to run a 100 mile race on her fifty-second birthday on October 15, 2005. What's next?

Addendum—7/2/05—Tamara completed the fifty-mile ultramarathon in Finger Lakes National Forest in 11:09:30. She was tenth of eighteen runners and had to contend with elevation changes of 2,000 feet, a bull giving her the evil eye, and a barb wire fence crossing. Good luck on the 100-miler, Tamara!

From the Crim to Flying Pigs

FRANK HAZEN

AGE: 37
YEARS RUNNING: 3
CRIM FINISHES: 3
YEARS IN CTP: 4
RESIDENCE: DAVISON, MI
OCCUPATION: CREDIT MANAGER

My "Crim Story" starts in 1997 when a co-worker asked if I was interested in joining the Crim Training Program. Being very out of shape, I never seriously considered running ten miles, at least not all in the same year.

She said, "Come on, you can do it. You walk a little, you run a little. It's easy."

After much persuasion, I said I would join the training program, and I did. It certainly wasn't easy at first, and it seemed like I was always the one at the back of the pack. Over the course of the summer, however, my group dragged me along, and I finished my first Crim.

I figured that because I had done it the first time, I'd be back every year to run the Crim. I started the training program again in 1998, but due to the time demands of graduate school, I wasn't able to complete the training or the Crim. After I got my master's degree in 1999, my first daughter was born in 2000. I changed jobs and was working out of town. Okay, enough with the excuses!

I got my next Crim inspiration in 2002 by taking my then two-year-old daughter to the Teddy Bear Trot. Watching the diversity of people of all ages, shapes, and sizes crossing the finish line, I told my wife that I was going to cross the finish line next year, even if I had to walk the entire way. I got really inspired when I saw the picture of myself helping my daughter cross the finish line of the Teddy Bear Trot. Let's just say it's my "before" picture.

In January 2003, I joined Weight Watchers and I started losing weight. Exercising and running became easier. By the time the Crim Training Program started in May, I had lost fifty-seven pounds. This year I enjoyed the program and was part of an excellent motivational training group. With diet and exercise, I had lost almost seventy pounds before the Crim.

Near the end of the Crim Training Program, one of my leaders asked if anyone in the group would like to continue training on Tuesday nights with the goal of running the Detroit Marathon in October. I never imagined I would run more than a ten-mile race; however, ultimately I said yes. He and I continued to train during the week and did our long runs on the weekends. On October 5, 2003, I ran my first marathon in 3:50:45. When I crossed the finish line, I honestly didn't know whether I was going to laugh or cry. I know my body was ready to cry. What an experience!

I had done it all. I had run the Crim twice, and I had run a marathon. I could kick back and relax, right? Wrong! I have since run the Las Vegas Marathon, the Cincinnati Flying Pig Marathon twice, and the Detroit Free Press Marathon twice.

I became a Crim Training Program group leader in 2004 with my former trainer from 2003. Yes, I still talk to him even after he encouraged me to start running marathons! We had a great group of runners and spent an enjoyable summer getting to know all of them and watching each person progress weekly. Five runners from our group ran fall marathons last year. It's funny how things come full circle.

What is the training program to me? It is a great motivational program that got me off the couch and physically fit. Running does get easier over time, and doing it alongside veteran runners gives you a great deal of insight into the sport. You learn what to wear, what not to wear, the right shoes, injury prevention, recovery, nutrition, hydration, and more. In the process you learn a lot about yourself.

As with anything that is not easy to do, training is much easier with the support of a group. When you know your group is there every Tuesday night, it is not as easy to find excuses not to go. You get to know the people in your group and other people in the program. You join races together, run together on other nights of the week or on the weekends, go for drinks or dinner after running, and such. I also run with a great running group that gets together every weekend year-round. Together we trudge through the rain, hail, sleet, snow, mud, and heat and love doing it.

Before I started running, I could never have imagined what it takes to mentally and physically prepare for the big day, whether that day is ten miles of running or 26.2. Now I know it's a lot of fun.

Frank and his wife reside in Davison, Michigan with their two daughters (currently Kids Crim Classic and Teddy Bear Trot runners). In addition to running, Frank enjoys traveling, camping, and working around his home.

CHAPTER SEVEN
Gone But Not Forgotten

REMEMBERING
DR.GEORGE SHEEHAN

BOB L. DALY

AGE: 72
YEARS RUNNING: 25
CRIM FINISHES: 25
RESIDENCE: FENTON, MI
OCCUPATION: OWNER MARATHON
  BURGLAR ALARM

My love affair with running began in the winter of 1979. I had never given it a thought until my physician suggested that I lose a few pounds, try to get my cholesterol down, and get my life back together. I had just become separated after a twenty-two-year marriage and was feeling a little sorry for myself. Dr. Abbott suggested that I give the YMCA exercise program a try.

The YMCA literally changed my life for the better. Back then, Randy Walker led a co-ed exercise class at the Y. After stretching, jumping jacks, and lunges, he had us jog around the gym. I'm sure that anyone in those classes will remember Frenchie Sullivan. He was instrumental in getting many runners on the road. One night after exercise class Frenchie was taking a few of the girls out for a run and asked if I might like to join them. I didn't know what I was in for.

"Just a couple of miles," the Frenchman said with a laugh.

After about two miles I was ready to stop and walk back to the YMCA. No dice. Frenchie would not let any of *his* runners quit.

"Not much farther," he teased as his tree-trunk thighs thundered along the road.

That night he proved to me that I could run, and in fact, finish five miles. That was it! I was hooked!

I started running regularly with other guys at the Y, including Wally McLaughlin, Bill LaFay, Ron Butler, Randy Walker and Clem Weierstahl. These YMCA veterans introduced me to racing, competition, and the fun that comes with running. At forty-seven-years-old I was running well, usually placing near the top in my age group. After my first few races, Ron Butler hung a nickname on me. I became known to the entire YMCA group as "Smoker Bob". By the way, the nickname wasn't because of impressive speed during my runs, but because after a race I jogged to the parking lot, opened up the truck, and grabbed a cigarette.

I kept running, winning, and smoking. As do all serious runners, I subscribed to *Runner's World* and learned that if I could quit smoking I could gain ten percent oxygen uptake and possibly run faster. That was it. Goodbye cigarettes, hello serious running competition. The nickname has followed me throughout my running career, and to this day, some twenty-five years later, Ron Butler still refers to me as "Smoker."

Since those eventful days of 1980 I have run five Detroit Free Press Marathons, one Chicago Marathon, one Flying Pig Marathon, and seventeen Boston Marathons. The Detroit Free Press was the first marathon I had ever run, and I finished with a time of 2:53 at the age of fifty-two. In April 1986 I ran my first Boston Marathon. I was fifty-three-years-old, and finished seventeenth in my age group out of 290 runners with a finishing time of 2:57:31. That first time in Boston did it; I fell in love with the challenging and prestigious course of the Boston Marathon.

As a surprise for me that year, my wife Luce, who is

a dental hygienist, had a dental lab technician cast a huge gold Boston Marathon ring for me. The dental lab melted down some of my wife's old gold jewelry and crowns and bridges we have had replaced throughout the years. You should see the ring. It looks like a football Super Bowl ring, complete with my initials, my first Boston time, and the year 1986. It is one of my most prized possessions.

In the 2004 Boston Marathon I took fifth place in the 70-and-over age group. My time was not the best for the marathons I have run, but the temperature at the start of the race was eighty-six degrees, and I am proud of my finish place, in spite of the treacherous weather conditions.

Meanwhile, I'll get back to the Crim in Flint, Michigan. I have always wanted to break one hour in the ten-miler, but I guess it just wasn't to be. My best finishing time in the ten-mile Crim Race was 1:01 when I was fifty-two years old. I just turned seventy-two years old on August 8, 2004, and this year will be my twenty-fifth consecutive ten-mile Crim road race.

All Crim races are special to me, but perhaps my most memorable Crim was in 1992. I had decided to run the ten-miler and then also run the 5K race back to back.

Coincidentally, Dr. George Sheehan was at the 1992 Crim Expo as a featured speaker. Dr. Sheehan, as many of you may recall, was not only an avid runner but also wrote many books on running and offered advice in *Runners World* magazine. I had read his books and articles and followed his running advice for years. There would be no chance of me missing his appearance at the expo.

After his message to the audience, he asked if we had any questions. My hand shot up like a rocket. I quizzed him in hopes of gaining expert insight on my anticipated back-to-back Crim races. It was going to be another hot, humid day for the festival of races. I wanted to be prepared for the battle between ten miles of pavement, legs, and pure guts, and be able to run a good 5K afterwards.

Dr. Sheehan seemed quite impressed at my goal. I suppose he was intrigued because I had recently turned sixty years old. He instructed me like a coach, to run the first race, the ten-miler, *like hell!* Come in, change into dry clothes, drink plenty of water, and sit in the shade of a big tree until the start of the 5K race.

I did as Dr. Sheehan instructed and ran the ten-miler like there was no tomorrow. I came in second in my age group, sixty to sixty-four, with a time of 1:07:31. After changing, rehydrating, and sitting under a tree on the lawn of the University of Michigan, I ran the 5K and took first place with a finishing time of 20:53. I was elated and grateful for the running guru's strict, no-nonsense counsel.

I wrote to Dr. Sheehan to thank him for his advice and to let him know that I indeed followed his suggestions and won top places in both the races. Graciously he wrote me back with congratulations, and of course, as was his way, more running advice.

Prior to the 1992 Crim race Dr. Sheehan had been diagnosed with cancer, and I think that was the last race he was able to run. With courage and his love for running, Dr. Sheehan ran and completed the ten-mile road race in the seventy to seventy-four age group with a time of 2:05:08. He had always been a great competitor in his age group, and this, his slowest of Crim times, is evidence of how he must have suffered that day during those endless ten miles. His pain and courage to run and finish ten miles while in the advanced stages of prostate cancer have been and always will be an inspiration to me.

I think about him and remember that Crim day in 1992, his love for running, and the motivation he gave me in those races. I will be running in the seventy to seventy-four age group this year, George's age group in his last courageous Crim race, and I will dedicate my race in 2004 to my running mentor, Dr. George Sheehan.

"George, I'm shooting for first place this year in the ten-miler, that is if that world-class Canadian, Ed Whitlock, first seventy-year-old to run a marathon under three hours and last year's ten-mile Crim time 1:02:28, stays across the river.

Addendum—8/28/04—"George, we did it! Thanks for all your running advice, my friend, it and you have become a very positive part of my life."

Bob Daly; first place, seventy to seventy-four age group in 1:19:27!

Bob and his wife Luce, own and operate Marathon Burglar Alarm. They install burglar and fire alarm protection in residential and commercial buildings. It's a bit alarming to me that all I ever get to see of Bob is the smoke coming off him as he moves off at seven-minute pace in local races. I never see him for long. Once he was having a bad day at a local 15K, and I almost caught him. Almost. Even if I had, he is more than thirty years ahead of me!

Bob's interest in historic lighting spawned another business and he buys, restores and sell antique lighting fixtures of all kinds. Luce works with Bob in both businesses. She is a dental hygienist in Swartz Creek, Michigan. In his spare time, Bob finds time to run and train for his favorite races. This August will mark his twenty-sixth consecutive ten-mile Crim race.

SLOW AND STEADY WINS THE RACE

TERESA SAXTON-MERRITT

TERESA   JANE   SUSAN

AGE: 44

YEARS RUNNING: 22

CRIM FINISHES: 17

YEARS IN CTP: 5

RESIDENCE: GRAND BLANC, MI

OCCUPATION: EMPLOYED AT
PRECISE PRODUCT ENGINEERS

When I ran the Crim for the first time, I was twenty-two years old. It was 1983, the year I graduated from college. Since then I have completed seventeen Crim ten-mile races. My brother Tom was my inspiration and one of the original ten-milers. Being a Flint native, I saw the Crim as a way to support the city and spend the day with my brother. In the years that have passed, I have been in the Crim Training Program as a participant and as a group leader.

Each year I began my routine in the spring. I would start my training and drag myself out the door, dreading the cold weather running. When I got back home I was fatigued and sore, but always wanted to push myself. I wanted to beat my running mates and was forever in pursuit of faster times. As I grew older, this became more of a challenge.

In 2004, my outlook on life changed. My sister

Carrie had been ill and died from a vascular tumor. Carrie was a forty-one-year-old mother of three. Although she never ran the Crim, she was very athletic and a competitive former MSU soccer player. During her six year battle with the illness, she endured three brain tumor surgeries, bone surgery, and radiation treatments. She eventually lost most of her sight and some of her hearing. Through all of this, she remained positive and upbeat. She was always interested in what was going on in the lives of others, despite her ordeal.

Carrie rarely complained and was hopeful and courageous to the end. Her motto was, "Slow and steady wins the race."

Her passing had an effect on the way I approached running. I surprised myself when I ran the Crim in 2004. I was encouraging my running mates as they passed me instead of being frustrated. I found myself thanking the many volunteers along the course, instead of keeping my nose to the ground. I was not worrying about the clock and instead focused on enjoying the moment.

In memory of Carrie, my whole family ran the Crim. My two sisters, Jane and Susan, finished their first ten-miler. My brother Tom finished his twentieth Crim. At the age of forty-three, I ran my slowest race ever, and learned that Carrie was right: "Slow and steady wins the race."

In memory of Carrie Saxton-Woods
12/13/63 – 1/10/04
Keep shining Carrie, we love you.

Teresa is married to Mathew Merritt and has two children, Jacob, age 14, and Sarah, age 10. She works at Precise Product Engineers, a dental hand piece repair company that is family owned and operated. She would like to thank her brother, Tom Saxton, for his role in encouraging her to become the athlete she is today. She sends special thanks to her angel Carrie, who was the inspiration for this story.

ED'S DEVIL OF A DEAL

RILEY MCLINCHA

AGE: 54
YEARS RUNNING: 29
CRIM FINISHES: ALL 28
YEARS IN CTP: 5
RESIDENCE: CLIO, MI
OCCUPATION: ENTERTAINER,
RETIRED GM TRADESMAN

I was driving on Longway heading downtown for the start of the 2005 Crim race. I had to stop at the light, the one by Mott College where the Crim used to start. Standing there in the traffic island was an old white-haired man. He was wearing a Crim race shirt from 1978 and polyester running shorts. I couldn't believe my eyes. The guy looked exactly like Ed Wiberg. He waved his arms and jumped up and down and was screaming, trying to get my attention. I rolled down my window.

"Where is everybody?" he yelled.

"Mister, you look lost." Deranged, I wanted to say.

"The Crim Race is s'posta to be today," he said.

"Well, yeah, but it doesn't start here; it hasn't started here in years." I felt bad for the old guy; he was obviously suffering from Alzheimer's.

"Can you take me to the start? I gotta get to the start," he said frantically.

"Sure, I'll take you to the start. Hop in." I was going to take him somewhere, all right, Hurley Hospital psych ward. "You look like a guy I used to know. What's your name?" I asked.

"I'm Ed Wiberg, back to run my last Crim," he stated.

"Well, you're a dead ringer for him for sure, but Eddie Wiberg ran his last Crim more than twenty years ago. If you're Ed, either I'm dreaming, or you're a ghost."

"You're neither. Just before I died I sold my soul to the devil with the agreement I could run the Crim one more time."

"That sounds like something Ed would do," I mumbled to myself.

As we passed Farmer's Market and crossed the Flint River, he continued. "But the devil can't be trusted; he's the devil I tell ya. After I signed on the dotted line, he pointed out the clause in the contract where he got to pick which Crim I got to run. I've been in Hell now for more than twenty years."

He sobbed. "Now he picks this Crim and doesn't even tell me where the start is. You know what's the worst part of being in Hell? They don't let you run! I told the devil that now I was in no shape to run ten miles.

"The devil laughed and said, 'You can die trying...oh wait...ha, ha, you're already dead! But I'll tell you what, since you have been here twenty years, if you can complete the entire Crim I will tear up our contract.' So you see I have hell to lose for trying."

We were nearing Saginaw Street. I had a decision to make: Do I continue to the hospital or turn and take him to the start? I pulled into the Rally's parking lot at the corner.

"Well, I half believe you. I remember Ed Wiberg, and if you aren't Ed, you're his clone," I mused.

"Oh, no, I'm no clown; I'm serious, dead serious, and I'm the real thing. So c'mon, where do we start?" said the ghost Ed.

"It starts downtown and finishes downtown. Much of the course is the same, just follow the blue line," I told him.

"The blue line, what's that?" he asked.

"It's right there," I told him, pointing to it across the street. "They started painting it after 1989, the year the lead vehicle missed the turn onto Chicago Avenue, which was almost a disaster. It almost cost Kathy O'Brien a national record."

"I don't know who she is and don't care. Let's worry about me," the ghost went on. With the importance of this race to him, I could see why he didn't care about the elite runners, but then he asked, "Who won the race last year?"

"Can't remember; some Kenyan is all I know."

"Steve Kenyon! He won it twice; don't tell me that S.O.B. is still winning it."

"No, this guy's from Kenya, the country. The winners are almost always from Africa."

"How big is the race now?"

"That depends on which race you're talking about," I said.

"I'm talking about the Crim, fool! What other race have we been talking about?"

"Well, if you say the Crim, you mean the ten-miler, but there's an 8K, 5K, one-mile, there are walking races, and a toddler's race. Man there are all kinds of races."

"They went and wrecked it. With that many races the ten-miler must have dwindled in size and prestige."

"I thought the same thing when they added the half Crim back in '87, but the ten-miler is still the premier event. Last year we had out biggest field, more than 6,500 finishers."

"Holy bejesus; we were getting only 2,000 before I croaked."

"Well, now it's called The Crim Festival of Races, and more than 14,000 people participate. It's still the biggest racing event in Michigan. Guess what Crim stands for?"

"Everybody better know what it stands for; it stands for my friend Bobby Crim, the man who created the race. Is he still around? Will I see him?"

"Yeah, he's still around; he's your age now and running as well as you did, around eighty-five minutes for ten miles."

"Oh, I did better than that! I ran eighty-one minutes when I was seventy-one, but I won't keep up with him today, I'm so out of shape." Ed shook his head.

"I was going to say Crim also stands for Coolest Race In Michigan, but not to worry; Bobby will not be forgotten; neither will Lois Craig and the original reason for the Crim: Michigan Special Olympics. The old timers like me will make sure of that. What's cool are the many things Crim means now besides a ten-mile race, thanks to the Crim Board of Directors. There is a Crim office downtown that's open year-round, not to mention the Crim Training Program for walkers and runners, the Crim Running Clubs for kids and teens, and the Crim Kids Classic. Why, the name Crim has become synonymous with fitness, not just in Genesee County, but throughout Michigan, and it's spreading further. Now that's cool. Don't cha think?" I said with Crim pride.

"Yeah, yeah, well I don't know anything about cool; I was never cool. C'mon, man, take me downtown. I still gotta enter. I don't wanna miss the start." He sounded a little cantankerous with his me, me, me attitude. Yep, this is the real Wiberg, I thought.

"This is probably the best parking place we'll get this late. C'mon, let's walk to the Character Inn. That's the Hyatt Regency to you; that's where you can sign up and get your chip." We got out, and I locked the doors.

"My chip?" Ed wondered.

"I'd explain it, but you wouldn't believe me. Let's just say you won't be getting a Popsicle stick at the finish line," I said with a hint of nostalgia.

We arrived downtown, and Ed could not believe all the people. At first he turned only a few heads. One head at the starting line had two eyes popping out.

"John! Hey, John Gault," Ed yelled. "I wanna start up front," Ed told him.

"Listen, you old coot, even if you are who you look like, you're not getting anywhere near the front," John said wisely.

"Listen here, mister! This ain't your race. Today it's

mine!" Ed barked.

I was beginning to think I'd made a big mistake bringing him downtown, but soon people who remembered him gathered. Moments later we were standing with Bobby Crim, Mark Bauman, Lois Craig, and more than twenty other old timers. He repeated his story that seemed like BS, but they bought it, the same as I did. We wanted to believe.

Deb Kiertzner, the race director took him to the MC platform. They climbed up, and Michael Dach, the MC, handed the mike to Deb. "Can I have everyone's attention..."

It took awhile, but before the race started, everyone heard Ed's story and understood why he had to finish. He gained the attention and support of 20,000 people. Far off, a block and a half away, a voice was heard: "Hell no, he won't go!" It caught on. With each repetition the number of voices doubled. It reverberated off the walls of the Character Inn, Citizen's Bank, and University Pavilion. The elite runners took a little longer to catch on, but soon they talked among themselves and they, too, began chanting, "Hell no, he won't go!" in many accents.

Ed hurriedly climbed down from the platform and into the crowd. As he moved to the front, runners gave him a wide berth and applauded rhythmically. He toed the starting line and looked directly at John Gault's stern face. John finally cracked a smile, shook his head, and joined the chanting. "Hell no, he won't go!"

The race started, and the Kenyans left Eddie in their dust. The field began passing him by the hundreds. It was a wonder he was not pushed to the pavement, with everyone slapping him on the back. I caught Ed myself at the first mile; his pace was 10:30.

I told him, "Ed, slow down. Take a walk break. It's the only way you will make it".

He griped, "Are you crazy? I'm a runner. Runners don't walk."

"It's OK, Ed, I haven't quite kicked that purist attitude myself, but remember what's at stake. You can do this if you use the Galloway Method."

"Galloway, Schmalloway, I ain't walking. Who is Galloway, anyway?" the curmudgeon yelled.

"Jeff Galloway; you remember, the Olympic runner. He takes walk breaks now," I said.

"Well, I'm no better than an Olympic runner. Hmmm, walking does sound real tempting right now."

"Hell, I'm telling you, it's the only way you'll make it. I mean, it's the only way you won't make it back to Hell. You'll be in good company today; hundreds of people will be walking and running. The Galloway Method is the reason for the second running boom," I told him.

Ed began walking. More and more people were matching his pace. By three miles he had a crowd surrounding him, all running two minutes then walking two. Spectators on the course were uninformed as to what was going on but knew something special was happening and cheered loudly. By six miles Ed had an army of believers with him. When the horde turned onto Miller near the eight-mile mark, ahead of him was a field with no runners. Runners were slowing down to run with Ed. Others, unaware of Ed behind them, continued onward. At the finish line fewer finishers were seen until only trickles of runners were coming in. Scott Hubbard, manning the P.A., went silent with no names to call out. He was the first to realize what was happening.

"Folks, the rest of the field is out there helping Ed Wiberg," he said with excitement.

His announcement nearly caused a stampede. Close to a thousand people in the downtown area headed back toward Court Street. They found Eddie's army near the White Horse Tavern and chanted, "Hell no, he won't go!" The multitude made the turn onto Saginaw Street. A block later Ed hit the bricks first. He began his last run interval. Everyone else marched behind him with fists in the air.

I yelled, "Stick it to the devil, Ed!"

Ed crossed the finish line, fell down, kissed the bricks, and stopped breathing.

John Gault was the first one to him. He shouted,

"Ed, you can't stop there, keep moving!"

Dr. Dan Walter, the closest medical person to him, touched Ed's face, which was cold as clay. "Eddie's dead," he disclosed.

Nobody was saddened, for Eddie had won his race. His final victory was over. Many continued to congratulate the corpse. "You did it, Ed. You beat the devil."

Predictably, when finish-line officials tried to move his body it disappeared.

This story is the only work of fiction that was submitted. For those unfamiliar with Ed Wiberg, he was Michigan runner of the year in 1980. The Crim was Ed's first road race and he finished the inaugural race in white dress shoes with platform heels. When he crossed the finish line in the ninety degree heat, people shook their heads in disbelief. Rumor has it that he started running at age seventy to help him quit drinking. He ran the first five Crims and he went on to set age-group time records in his late seventies. After Ed passed on in 1989 he was buried in his 1977 Crim T-shirt. Local veteran runners ran along behind the hearse to his funeral. Now that's a runner!

CHAPTER EIGHT
Bonus Chapter

WHY RUN, IF NO ONE IS CHASING YOU?

ANTHONY ELLIS, M.D.

One of the interesting common threads that run through the stories in this book involves stepping outside of a comfort zone and into something new. The people who wrote these personal reflections for others to read had an interest in celebrating the agent of change that running had become for them. Their initial curiosity led to a new health-sustaining habit that was fun and rewarding physically as well as emotionally. Two major reasons they were able to navigate the "three-month hump" that stops most would-be exercisers were group support and a structured program. Starting a new exercise regimen on your own is not the same as training for an attainable goal with a group. The group greatly enhances the chance for success and reduces dropout rates, as I found out myself.

The reason I wanted to collect these accounts of transformation was to promote planned group exercise as a means to an end. The endpoint is taking control of your physical and psychological health. No one else can do it for you. If you want to increase your functional lifespan, improve your level of happiness and self confidence, and protect your brain from the ravages of time, you must exercise and eat a healthy diet. Everyone knows these truths, but few act on this vital information.

Through my work as a geriatric psychiatrist, I see the end results of poor health habits. The combination of inactivity, poor diet, inadequate self care, and high levels of stress culminate in premature aging of the body and mind. One has only to walk around the inpatient psychiatry unit where I work to see the fate potentially awaiting each of us. The suffering for patients and families is palpable to the treatment team that helps me do what we can for the people we treat. The hopeful thing about declining function with age is that some of it is preventable with exercise, diet, and stress reduction.

New studies show that you can begin at almost any age and still improve your overall health, extend the longevity of your mind, and extend your functional life in the process. If the stories in this book don't get you fired up and off the couch, perhaps some information about the consequences of inactivity will spark the fire under your well-cushioned caboose. Exercise your mind with these daunting statistics and information about the current state of affairs in Michigan and the United States as a whole. The data presented here are for illustrating trends, as these numbers change yearly and are not always available for the current year.

- About 2/3 of Americans are overweight

- About 1/4 of Americans are obese

- Michigan is one of the five states with the highest percentage of obese residents. (24.4%)

- Common conditions associated with obesity include premature death, high blood pressure, arthritis, cancer, cardiovascular disease, and diabetes.

- More than a quarter of Americans will die of cardiovascular disease. It is the number-one cause of death after age 65 and is number two from age 45 to 64.

- An estimated 400,000 deaths in the United States each year are attributable to lack of adequate exercise. This number is comparable to the 435,000 annual deaths attributable to smoking.

- Around 25 percent of Americans report no exercise at

all, and a sedentary lifestyle reportedly increases risk of stroke by 400 percent. Stroke is the number-three cause of death for people over age 65.

• Almost half of young Americans between the ages of 12 and 21 do not engage in regular physical exercise.

• Americans think they are healthier than they actually are. More than 60 percent of Americans don't exercise enough to yield health benefits.

• More than 21 percent of Americans still smoke, and chronic lung disease is the fourth leading cause of death after age 65.

• Compared to a normal body mass index a BMI of 30 to 35 correlates with double the risk for coronary artery disease, high blood pressure, and osteoarthritis. It quintuples the risk for type 2 diabetes in men and triples the risk for type 2 diabetes for women.

• Two-thirds of people with a BMI of 40 have high blood pressure. This level of obesity carries about a 15 percent risk of *each* of these chronic health conditions: type 2 diabetes, coronary artery disease, and osteoarthritis.

To calculate your body mass index use this non-metric formula:

CALCULATING YOUR BODY MASS INDEX

$$BMI = \frac{WEIGHT\ IN\ POUNDS}{HEIGHT\ IN\ INCHES \times HEIGHT\ IN\ INCHES} \times 703$$

BELOW 18.5 . . . . UNDERWEIGHT

18.5 TO 24.9 . . . . NORMAL

25 TO 29.9 . . . . OVERWEIGHT

OVER 30 . . . . OBESE

OVER 40 . . . . MORBIDLY OBESE

BMI is only one predictor of risk for certain health conditions. Other factors to consider are blood pressure, blood sugar, blood cholesterol, level of exercise, family history, and diet. In addition, some athletes with a large amount of muscle mass have an increased BMI, but may be in excellent condition.

The plain and simple truth is that many chronic health conditions have common denominators. They are: lack of exercise, poor diet, smoking, obesity, and the effects of excess stress.

The good news about running and walking is that almost anyone can do one or the other. They don't cost much. You can even do them indoors when the weather requires. They also induce secondary changes in health awareness and self image, increase the focus on needed dietary changes, and reduce stress. For example, no one in my running group smokes. They don't drink to excess, and they make better food choices. As a rule, they have lost weight or gained muscle mass, changing their metabolism. They have also had the benefits of a supportive group of like-minded individuals to help them during stressful times.

Exercise has been shown to reduce blood pressure, lower "bad" cholesterol, induce weight loss, and produce net muscle gain. Weight-bearing exercise increases bone density and reduces the risk of osteoporosis. Running increases VO2, which is a measure of maximum oxygen uptake. This parameter decreases with age, but the decline is slower in physically active people. The better your VO2, the better your body functions and the slower you show your age. The age-related decline in muscle mass with age is also slowed by active exercise such as running. If you want to do well in your later years, invest in your level of conditioning now and develop an exercise routine for the rest of your life.

You don't have to run fast to get the calorie-burning benefits. The determining factor in calories-burned-per-mile is more related to the runner's weight than running pace. Here is one place where weight helps. The more you weigh, the more calories you will burn at a given pace. Walking burns about half as many calories per mile, so you have to invest twice as much time, but the overall benefits are similar. Racewalking provides the benefits of running without the knee and joint pounding that can be difficult for people with bad knees or back problems. If you can't walk, you can exercise in a pool, or on a bike, or on an elliptical trainer.

Runners report higher levels of personal satisfaction and lower stress levels. The psychological benefits of running outpace the physical stress encountered when beginning a running program. Running helps reduce tension, fatigue, and insomnia. Some studies suggest that running and aerobic exercise in general can be an effective antidepressant for many people with mild to moderate depression. Several recent studies show that exercise improves mental health by helping the brain better cope with stress. The anxiety-reducing benefits of running may have a protective effect on brain health by reducing levels of cortisol, the stress hormone, which has been shown to damage brain cells and impair memory function.

Other body functions decline with age. Sexual function can become an issue for middle-aged men and women unless they take care of their circulatory systems. Sexual dysfunction is more common in those with poor overall health. Vigorous exercise can be effective in reducing impotence. In one study, the benefits were seen with walking as little as two miles daily or exercising enough to burn around 200 calories. Another study took sedentary males and had them exercise three to four hours a week. The study participants reported improvements in potency, frequency of sex, and increased levels of satisfaction. People feel better about themselves when they are in shape, and their improved self confidence and healthier body image translates into better sex. Active men are less likely to have impotence problems. You can help keep your sexual functioning intact by having normal body weight, quitting smoking, and reducing excess alcohol intake. All of these changes frequently result from becoming a runner or participating in an exercise program.

Exercise and sensible caloric restriction improve longevity. These claims are no longer disputed. A study of more than 17,000 Harvard University alumni from 1962 to 1995 showed that exercise was inversely related to death rates. The people who exercised the most did the best, on average. Other studies on the effects of exercise have shown a 40 percent reduction in risk of heart attack in women and 60 percent reduction in heart attacks in men. The group of people in the lowest 20 percent for cardiovascular fitness had a death rate three times higher than the fit group. Exercise has a logarithmic effect on health because of the *synergy* between increased cardiovascular health, lower weight, lower cholesterol, stress reduction, and improved self image.

Some of the most exciting recent data available about exercise and brain health suggests that exercise stimulates brain chemicals that protect new brain cells. This protein, called "brain-derived neurotrophic factor," helps brain cells grow and make new connections. This news is especially interesting to those of us working with patients suffering from Alzheimer's disease. The memory-boosting effects of running have been shown to protect the hippocampus, the area of the brain affected earliest in patients afflicted with Alzheimer's. Older adults who exercise have brains that are more densely packed with extra connections and are more resistant to damage. The studies show not only preserved function, but also actual improvement. These new studies suggest that we may be able to delay the onset of this terrible disease. The link may have to do with reducing vascular damage in the brain related to poor oxygen delivery. By reducing the "clogged-blood-vessel-related" damage, people will not show symptoms until a later age and may have more functional years.

All right, that's enough. If you are still on the couch, I can't get you up. I could go on about the health benefits of running or walking or exercise in general, but that's another book. Besides, I've got to get outside and run! Good luck to you and yours. I hope you live long and well.

I'll see you at the races. I'll be the guy with the matching running clothes wearing a GPS running watch and listening to an MP3 player.

Anthony R. Ellis, M.D.
June 2005

Appendix

EVOLUTION OF THE CRIM POSTER

From 1977 to 1979, Ben Titus, an artist on the Democratic House Communication staff in Lansing, Michigan, designed the poster. It featured the world-class winner from the previous year and space for Special Olympics, the host-city of Flint, and major sponsors.

From 1979 until 1982, Ron Butler and his marketing department from Genesee Bank, now known as Bank One, designed the poster. For the first time, graphics were used to design the stick figure, and then were slightly altered from year to year.

The Democratic House Communication staff once again designed the poster in 1983. The design featured a watercolor depiction of Joan Benoit racing to her first Crim victory surrounded by Special Olympics athletes.

Ben Titus donated his talents once again and designed the poster in 1984.

The 1985 poster designed by a Hurley Medical Center artist named Beccial was a big hit. The poster depicts a photo of well-worn running shoes hanging on a locker. Quite different from previous posters, it proved very popular with Crim runners.

The Crim celebrated its tenth year in 1986. Dee Knott, an American watercolor artist from Flushing, Michigan, designed the 1986 poster. Knott's poster was and is the most sought after Crim poster to date. Her renowned talents brought a full-colored poster packed with speed drama called "Ribbons of Victory." She designed the work from a photo she had taken at the finish line the previous year. Dee inserted elements she sensed best represented the Crim; a wheeler, her vision of Crim runners, international flags on the finish line representing the international status of the race, a female runner, and the red bricks of Saginaw Street. Knott designed the Crim T-shirts for several years, achieving the first national award for design from *Runner's World* magazine.

In 1988, the art department of Mott Community College was approached to compete in a poster design contest. Among the original works that were created, Brian Kaldahl's was selected as the Crim poster for that year. The poster displayed a pair of running shoes with its laces spelling Crim.

Karl Olmsted began designing the Crim poster in 1989. He introduced the energetic, Keith Herring-inspired running figure that holds a sun-beaming "C" above his head. Olmsted also used differently shaped running and background figures. By 1996, the running figure underwent intriguing shape changes through the work of Andrew Ward, an artist at Olmsted Associates. The changes allowed new exciting figures and designs. Ward has designed the Crim poster and T-shirt from 1992 to 2005. Ward also designed the cover of this book.

Submitted by the Crim Organization

Chapter header pages and cover design showcase Crim poster art. I would like to express thanks to the Crim for letting me use these images. I would also like to extend special thanks to the original designers of these works of art that were created for, and donated to the Crim by the artists.

Spirit Of The Crim (Hit The Bricks)

By Riley McLincha

It started with a man, whose idea became the plan
Helping special people know no limitations
And today where we stand his dream is in our hands
We're on the road beyond expectations

Brick by brick the dream has grown
To hearts and souls of young and old
Reaching new horizons with passing of the years
Oh when you see those bricks my friend oh push to the end
Cross the line and join the celebration
See the pride on every face in this human race
Hit the bricks and feel the spirit of the Crim

Come run or walk or cheer or come and volunteer
Come witness fruits of will and dedication
Come follow the trail where charity prevails
We're on the road beyond expectations

Community involvement and world participation
Oh they're building blocks of hope for our foundation
And when you see those bricks my friend push to the end
Cross the line and join the celebration
See the pride on every face in this human race
Hit the bricks and feel the spirit of the Crim
Hit the bricks and feel the spirit of yeah
The spirit of the Crim

In Recognition of More Than 25 Years

VOLUNTEERS

Ric Hogerheide
Mark Bauman
Elliott Deyo
Don Sweet

Jon Schriner
Peg Deyo
John Gault

Jan Nieuwenhuis
Downtown Flint
  Kiwanis Club

SPONSORSHIPS

Phil Shaltz – Shaltz Fluid Power
Genesee County Sheriff Dept.
Ron Butler – Bank One
Citizens Bank

City of Flint
UAW Local 598
UAW Local 651

RUNNERS

Mark Bauman
Robert Nelson
Ray Fielder
Jack Price
Gary Guerrieri
Phil Shaltz
Eric Jones
Norman Werth
Thomas Martin

Dan Miglin
Lance Dunbar
Robert Pickell
Timothy Giles
David Sanders
Charles Jackson
Daniel Walter
Thomas Galley
Riley McLincha

Kenn Domerese
Timothy Parker
James Forshee
Richard Ruddy
Terry Heany
Michael Vance
Ray Knott
Conrad Reinhard
Darrell McKee

ABOUT THE EDITOR

Dr. Ellis lives in Flushing, Michigan, with his wife Shari, and three daughters, Alaina, Serena, and Mia. By day he is a mild-mannered medical director of an inpatient geriatric psychiatry unit in Lansing, Michigan. Dr. Ellis works with a dedicated team of professionals delivering care to older adults on the G.E.M.S. Unit of Ingham Regional Medical Center. On his time off, he is an avid runner and writer. Dr. Ellis hopes to share his passion for running and its effects on brain health and longevity through his writing.

RUNNING THE CRIM
Stories from the Coolest Race In Michigan
Order Form

Fax orders: 810-600-I-RUN (4786). Send this form.

Telephone orders: Call 1-866-WHY-I-RUN (949-4786) toll free. Have your credit card ready.

E-mail orders: Orders@RunningBrain.com

Postal Orders: Make checks payable to Running Brain, LLC, and mail to: Running Brain, LLC, P.O. Box 320074, Flint, MI 48532

Name: _____

Address: _____

City: _____ State: _____

Zip: _____ Phone: _____

E-mail: _____

_____ Copies of book @ $14.95 each

$_____ Shipping ($4 first book and $2 each additional)

$_____ 6% Sales tax (for residents of Michigan)

$_____ Total Amount Due

MasterCard: _____ or VISA: _____

Card Number: _____ Exp. Date: _____

Name on card if different from above (please print clearly):

_____

Mine's running. Is yours?